FISH OR CUT BAIT

Fish or Cut Bait

How Winning Churches Make Decisions

John E. Kaiser

Foreword by Dan Southerland
Illustrations by Ruth Kaiser

Abingdon Press
Nashville

FISH OR CUT BAIT
HOW WINNING CHURCHES MAKE DECISIONS

Library of Congress Cataloging-in-Publication Data

Kaiser, John Edmund.
  Fish or cut bait : how winning churches make decisions / John E. Kaiser ; foreword by Dan Southerland ; illustrations by Ruth Kaiser.
    p. cm.
  Includes bibliographical references (p.   ).
  ISBN 978-1-4267-0064-4 (trade pbk. : alk. paper)
  1. Church management. 2. Decision making—Religious aspects—Christianity. I. Title.
  BV652.K25 2011
  254—dc22

                                                                                  2011015816

11 12 13 14 15 16 17 18 19 20—10 9 8 7 6 5 4 3 2 1

MANUFACTURED IN THE UNITED STATES OF AMERICA

This book is dedicated to

God's precious gift to me,

fashioned so perfectly,

to be held tenderly,

Leonore.

Remember when I wrote you that song?

Acknowledgments

MY WIFE, LEONORE, IS MY BIGGEST fan, though surely my least objective. If it were not for her patience, support, and helpful suggestions, however, this book would not have been written. Our daughter, Ruth, produced a terrific set of illustrations for chapters 2 through 6. You did a goooood job!

I would also like to thank my editor at Abingdon Press, Kathy Armistead. She requested this book from me initially and displayed incredible long-suffering as I asked for extension after extension to complete it.

My appreciation goes out to each of the leaders who spoke with me about their ministries over the couple of years leading up to this book. Some of you realized you might show up in print, and some of you didn't. I've done my best to cast your good work in a positive light and to obscure the bits that might create blowback for you or for others with whom you serve.

Edmund Kaiser Jr., my father, passed away between the publication of my first book and the writing of this one. The pride in me that he expressed will always mean a great deal. It feels a little strange not to know what he would say about *Fish or Cut Bait*. I can guess, though. I think about him every day.

Finally, my heartfelt thanks to those men and women who supported me through thick and thin in two pastorates over fifteen years, and to those pastors and colleagues who taught me so much as a consultant and denominational executive over the ten years that followed. I am indebted to you for the lessons in this book.

Contents

everybody has a list — the church in Acts was winning — consider three essentials — which is most important? — there are better questions — where this book is going — summary and preview

PART ONE—First Get the Big Questions Right

big choices make hard choices easier — the trap of paper values — the trap of values in a vacuum — introducing the big five questions — summary and preview

good decisions are driven by mission — cracking into the neighborhood — off the wall is on the mark — you shape the building, then it shapes you — sometimes you can't afford to keep the money — know when to hold 'em; know when to fold 'em — summary and preview

good decisions aim to please Christ — what's in a name? — sometimes your knees knock — if you must predict, predict often — integrity calls for courage — to please the Owner, find out what he wants — summary and preview

good decisions support the pastor's leadership — what gets in the way of strong leadership? — the nearest competing value —

PART TWO—Then Get the Devil Out of the Details

Foreword

IF YOU DON'T ASK THE RIGHT QUESTIONS, you don't get the right answers.

Someone must have impressed that into my limited brain at a very early age. I have always asked questions! I have always sought information. I have always believed that curiosity is a virtue.

The word *question* is derived from the Latin *quarrier* ("to seek"), which is the same root as the word for *quest*. Good questions become our guides to lead us to the right answers we so desperately need.

Most church leaders today are on a quest. They want to lead their flocks to become winning churches. They desire to see their people make a difference in the twenty-first-century world in which we live. They want all God has for them and for their people. They desire to see others come to love and become like and share Jesus. *Fish or Cut Bait* is written for those church leaders who are willing to wrestle through the tough questions in order to become all God wants them to be.

I honestly believe there is a good chance that John Kaiser and I were twins who were separated at birth. I got the good looks. John got the good brains. And we both got a huge dose of curiosity. John is a question asker! He is driven to find practical answers for himself and to share those practical answers with other church leaders who are on the same quest.

I always learn when I am with John. I know I can ask my questions without fear of reproach or rebuff. I know he will give me whatever wisdom he has and point me in the right direction for me to continue my quest. I know that his answers do not come from theory but from years of practice.

There is an interesting passage from the book of Job. God says to Job, "I have some questions for you, and you must answer them" (Job 42:4 NLT). I truly believe that when we stand before God, those of us who had the privilege of serving as leaders in God's church will give an account for how we lead.

In the years after I wrote *Transitioning: Leading Your Church through Change*, I had the privilege of speaking to more than one hundred thousand church leaders in hundreds of conference settings. I became convinced of two realities. The good news is that most church leaders want to lead their churches well. The bad news is that most church leaders do not have a clue how to make good decisions.

If you are ready to learn new paradigms and practices in how to make good decisions as you lead your church, I have great news. This book is for you! It's time to *Fish or Cut Bait*.

Dan Southerland
Author of *Transitioning: Leading Your Church through Change*
Lead Teaching Pastor, Westside Family Church, Kansas City, Kansas

Preface

If I had eight hours to chop down a tree,
I'd spend six hours sharpening my ax.
Abraham Lincoln

"I'VE EXPERIENCED ENOUGH SUCCESS SO that people will listen to me, and I've experienced enough failure so that I know what I'm talking about." That's a line I've used at training presentations from time to time. It's the truth—even if I did steal it from some other thief.

The research underlying *Fish or Cut Bait* is a combination of three decades of observing colleagues in professional ministry, my own experience as the lead pastor of a large church, ten years of consultations with hundreds of congregations from different tribes, and a recent look at a selected set of what I call "winning churches." The result of sifting and weighing my take on a host of successes and failures is the book you hold in your hands.

The saying "Fish or cut bait" appears to have its origin in the United States prior to the Civil War and has always referred in one way or another to making a clear choice.[1] One connotation of this fishing metaphor is an emphasis on selecting either one valuable contribution to make (catch fish) or another equally valuable contribution (prepare to catch fish). This meaning assumes that cutting bait refers to chopping dead fish into smaller pieces that can attract live ones. The other connotation of the metaphor is an emphasis on doing a task decisively (if you're going to fish, fish) or else withdrawing decisively (if you're not going to fish, stop going through the motions). This second meaning may assume that cutting bait refers to snipping the line to let a minnow or shrimp swim away if not needed.

Both connotations work well for decision making in the church context, especially when combined with Jesus' own metaphor for his disciples as fishermen of a new kind.[2] "The Son of Man came to seek and to save what was lost" (Luke 19:10), he said of his own purpose in the world. And those who would follow him would learn to do likewise. Congregations are groups of disciples. As such, they are to carry on the same outwardly focused purpose today. And so the metaphor works in one sense to say: *we need to evangelize, and we need to equip ourselves to evangelize. Let's decide which one we're about at the moment and do it right.* The other sense of the metaphor works as well: *if we are here to reach people for Christ, then let's get serious about it; if not, then let's stop calling ourselves disciples.* Fish or cut bait!

Christians gather to worship and to reach out in a host of patterns, not all of which are highly structured. American humorist Will Rogers said, "I'm not a member of any organized political party. I'm a Democrat." An increasing number of believers in recent years are opting out of what some of them derisively call "the I.C." (Institutional Church). Rather than hang out in auditoriums and fellowship halls, they hang out in cafés and living rooms. Some simply drop out altogether. *Fish or Cut Bait* will have less direct relevance to antiorganizational folk, but it should still speak to values that make a difference for serious Christians everywhere on the spectrum, from anarchists to antidisestablishmentarians.[3] (I've always wanted to use that word in a sentence, haven't you?)

Many of the particular practices recommended for and against in this book pertain to the use of nonprofit corporations as vehicles for ministry endeavors. Even the avant-garde for whom *evil corporation* is a redundant term tend to make use of corporations in practice for most of their activities that involve money. Some of these groups are incorporated but speak as if they are not. Others set up corporations on the side that are not accountable either to a body of believers or to a denomination. Most congregations, however, do use the common organizational tools of our culture to keep their work in good order. This vast majority has the most to gain from reading *Fish or Cut Bait.*

Most of the winning churches referenced throughout the book, and all of the ten profiled in the appendix, are either large, very large, or megachurches. This criterion does not imply that congregations of small (below two hundred members) and medium (two hundred to four hundred members) size cannot be healthy, growing churches. It implies instead that a congregation experiencing healthy, sustained growth will become a larger church in time, and that evidence over time is a part of choosing a model of success. Small churches don't need models to learn how to stay small; that's their default destiny unless they learn to think bigger. Congregations named as winners in *Fish or Cut Bait* were selected to reflect a variety of larger sizes, of denominations, of locations, of polities, and of cultures. Some examples in the book have missing or altered details to protect people in sensitive situations.

As its subtitle, *How to Organize Congregations to Succeed in Their Mission*, implies, my first book, *Winning on Purpose*, laid out a particular organizational strategy, one that I call "Accountable Leadership." It was presented through a game metaphor with three elements (object of the game, rules, and how to keep score) and four players (congregation for ministry, board for governance, pastor for leadership, and staff for management).

Fish or Cut Bait is not a study of congregations employing Accountable Leadership per se, although four of the ten profiled do happen to be using my model. The present book is a broader study of congregations that use some kind of structure that supports effective pastoral leadership, which is by no means limited to the one I presented in *Winning on Purpose*.

I have already noted the benefits that groups eschewing formal organization may gain from this book. As for the majority of churches that do use a nonprofit corporation, let's consider how the material may benefit a variety of sizes. Thriving megachurches (not all are) do not need this book. They may benefit from a few tactical suggestions, but for the most part they have a lead pastor who could write a decent book on the topic. One purpose that *Fish or Cut Bait* may serve for them, however, is to give them a handy resource for influencing congregations and leaders who seek their help. On the other end of the line are small congregations, those numbering fewer than 150 in worship attendance. They may find it hard to relate to many of the larger church examples in this book. Nevertheless, I would say to them that if they are willing to leave small-church thinking behind, they could attract pastors able to lead them to bigger things. There are two size ranges that should benefit most from *Fish or Cut Bait*. One is medium-size churches of about 150 attendees (where members need to learn trust) to 400 attendees (where boards need to learn trust). The other is large and very large churches from about 400 to 1,800 attendees. If they want to thrive, these kinds of congregations can see their immediate best future in many of the examples in this book.

Regardless of size, tongue, tribe, or style, if your congregation wants to go fishing in deeper waters for a spiritual catch, my prayer is that *Fish or Cut Bait* will fit nicely in your tackle box.

John E. Kaiser
Ontario, Canada

Introduction

*The problems of victory are more agreeable
than those of defeat, but they are no less difficult.*
Winston Churchill

THE YEAR 2017 WILL BE A BIG ONE FOR Canada. Count on it. How do I know? Because I was living there in 2007 and witnessed on Canadian television the ninetieth anniversary of the Battle of Vimy Ridge. Elizabeth II, queen of Canada, led the commemoration at the World War I battlefield memorial in Pas de Calais, France, alongside Prime Minister Harper. Yes, Canada has a queen; this is news to most Americans and to not a few Canadians. And you can bet that she or her successor will show up for the centennial as well.

Vimy Ridge was a pivotal battle in the Great War. It was the first Allied victory in nearly two years and offered the first hope of an eventual success over the kaiser and the Central Powers. The United States had entered the war only three days before the battle began and would take another year to fully enter the fighting. To understand the importance of this battle for Canada—a brigade commander leading the assault called it "the birth of a nation"—one must consider the immensity of the objective and the limitations of the Canadian military experience.

As a confederation, Canada was scarcely fifty years old in 1917, and its military was still treated as an adjunct to the British Expeditionary Force. Vimy was the first time that the four divisions of the Canadian Corps were brought together to execute a major operation. The Allies had all but given up on ever taking the triple German fortifications along Vimy Ridge. In 1915 alone, the French army had lost a staggering 150,000 men in the attempt. However, through a combination of tactical innovations and a weeklong bombardment (one million shells), the Canadians were able to take the objective in a mere three days following Easter Sunday. One such innovation was to build and rehearse on a scale model of the

1

Vimy defenses. Another was mastery of the "creeping barrage," by which infantry advanced behind a moving curtain of artillery fire. A third innovation was master-plan briefing with maps at the platoon level so that small units could improvise and adapt even if officers and communication lines were taken out in the heat of battle.

Brilliant stuff in theory, and, even better, it worked. Nor was the victory temporary. In fact, Canada still holds that ground today. Five years after the battle, in grateful recognition, France ceded 250 acres on Vimy Ridge to Canada as a permanent possession. The expansive memorial, completed in 1936, is on Canadian soil bought with Canadian blood.

What gives Vimy Ridge its mythic power in the collective psyche of Canadians? It was a daunting mission, one of utmost importance, and, against all odds—drumroll, please—the good guys won. David fought smart and Goliath fell hard.

The Church of the Lord Jesus Christ is engaged in spiritual, not physical, warfare. Its weapons are words of life rather than instruments of death. Its prisoners are not taken captive but set free. How can we determine whether our unit, the congregation we serve, is winning or losing? What would a Vimy-esque victory look like and feel like in pursuit of God's mission for his Church?

Everybody has a list

When it comes to the notion of success in the context of the church, there is no shortage of contenders. At one end of the spectrum are those for whom the very idea of success in the church is inappropriate, a corruption of authentic Kingdom values imported from the age of modernity. At the other end are those for whom victory in all things at all times is the birthright of believers, be it health, prosperity, or organizational expansion. Between the poles are those who, as a response to the question of success, seek in various ways to define "church health." What does a good, strong, prevailing, God-honoring, successful, spiritual, biblical, growing, New Testament, missional, healthy, great, Spirit-filled, thriving, or winning church look like? Pick whatever adjective makes you think "two thumbs up" about the church and try to answer the question. What you'll soon discover is that everybody has a list. Let's peruse several of those most widely published and used.

German theorist Christian Swartz, author of *Natural Church Development* and its spin-off materials, proposes eight essential qualities. He bases them on statistical research for correlation of their presence with growth and of their absence with decline. His primary conclusion is that churches with a score of 65 percent or better for each and every quality will grow automatically and naturally.

1. Empowering leadership
2. Gift-oriented ministry
3. Passionate spirituality
4. Functional structures
5. Inspiring worship service
6. Holistic small groups
7. Need-oriented evangelism
8. Loving relationships[1]

Stephen Macchia suggests the following ten characteristics in his book *Becoming a Healthy Church*. They were developed through discussions and surveys conducted by Vision New England whereby participants affirmed each characteristic's significance.

1. God's empowering presence
2. God-exalting worship
3. Spiritual disciplines
4. Learning and growing in community
5. A commitment to loving and caring relationships
6. Servant-leadership development
7. An outward focus
8. Wise administration and accountability
9. Networking with the body of Christ
10. Stewardship and generosity[2]

Kennon Callahan, out of his professional consulting and research with more than a thousand churches over some thirty years, developed a list he published in book form as *Twelve Keys to an Effective Church*.

1. Specific, concrete missional objectives
2. Pastoral and lay visitation
3. Corporate, dynamic worship
4. Significant relational groups
5. Strong leadership resources
6. Streamlined structure and solid, participatory decision making
7. Several competent programs and activities
8. Open accessibility
9. High visibility
10. Adequate parking, land, and landscaping
11. Adequate space and facilities
12. Solid financial resources[3]

The three lists above represent widely used criteria popularized by those whose base of knowledge and experience is primarily theoretical and analytical. Leading practitioners, pastors of large influential congregations, have produced other lists for church health and success. Here are three examples of that type.

Rick Warren, senior pastor of Saddleback Community Church in Southern California, is well known throughout and beyond the world of Christian publishing and speaking for his five purposes, applied first to the congregation in *The Purpose-Driven Church* and then to individuals in *The Purpose-Driven Life*. One iteration of his list takes the following form under the heading "Five Dimensions of Church Growth":

1. Churches grow warmer through fellowship.
2. Churches grow deeper through discipleship.
3. Churches grow stronger through worship.
4. Churches grow broader through ministry.
5. Churches grow larger through evangelism.[4]

Leith Anderson, senior pastor of Wooddale Church near Minneapolis and president of the National Association of Evangelicals, offers the following signs of health in *A Church for the 21st Century*:

1. Glorify God
2. Producing disciples
3. Exercise of spiritual gifts
4. Relating positively to one's environment
5. Reproduction
6. Incorporation of newcomers
7. Being openness to change
8. Trusting God and prayer[5]

Mark Dever, senior pastor of Capitol Hill Baptist Church in Washington, D.C., led the recovery of a church once numbering in the thousands that had dwindled down to one hundred members by the time he was called in 1994. Weekly attendance has since grown back to six hundred to eight hundred, including more than two hundred visitors. His list of criteria, presented intentionally as a biblical corrective to others that he views as overly pragmatic and growth oriented, was published in his book *Nine Marks of a Healthy Church*.

1. Expositional preaching
2. Biblical theology
3. Biblical understanding of the good news
4. Biblical understanding of conversion
5. Biblical understanding of evangelism
6. Biblical understanding of church membership
7. Biblical church discipline
8. Promotion of church discipleship and growth
9. Biblical understanding of leadership[6]

These six examples only scratch the surface. The pastor of a teaching church who has led a congregation through significant growth to the point of hosting a conference for other leaders eager to learn what worked, will understandably create a list of success criteria. With no fewer than twelve hundred Protestant megachurches in the United States alone, there are probably scores, if not hundreds, of such lists generated by leading practitioners, not to mention those published by consultants and leadership gurus. What can we learn from these kinds of lists? Quite a lot, actually.

First of all, each item on every list is the product of thoughtful reflection by a leader or analyst with a base of experience, either deep or wide. As such, each item is worth the consideration of pastors and teams seeking to learn from the happy minority of congregations in North America that are neither stuck on a plateau or sliding off in decline. Some of the listed criteria are means (e.g., "functional structures"), while others are outcomes (e.g., "glorify God"). Some of them are biblical mandates (e.g., "stewardship and generosity"), while others are cultural expectations (e.g., "adequate parking, land, and landscaping"). Virtually all of these criteria—considered individually—are helpful to local church leadership, at the very least for thinking through decisions.

A second learning opportunity stems from the fact that, when taken as a whole, each list reflects the philosophical bias of its creator. This observation is not meant as a criticism but as a prelude to deeper insight and more effective application for churches that use these lists. Whether the source of criteria is represented as clinical ("This is what worked for us, so I know what I'm talking about"), statistical ("This is what we found in more than a thousand churches on several continents and the numbers don't lie"), or theological ("Here are the nine marks of a healthy church; they are biblical, so end of discussion"), human interpretation of the source is unavoidable. The very biases of the list makers, however, can help a pastor grapple with ministry challenges through more than one pair of mental spectacles. For Warren, for instance, it's all about being obedient to God's purpose. For Dever, it's about being faithful to biblical theology. For Swartz, it's about an empirical formula for natural development. Which set of lenses do you need? Try each of them on and see which one or combination improves your vision. Better one . . . or two?

A third way of learning from the plethora of lists for a healthy church is to take a step back from them and ask some broad questions of comparison. For example, how many of the criteria on a given list are essentially inward, concerned with what happens inside the congregation, and how many are outward, concerned with the impact of the congregation on its mission field? Are the criteria in a given list weighted, or are they equal in importance? If I were to compose my own list of criteria for an effective congregation, what would I choose as a starting point?

The church in Acts was winning

To understand the concept of a successful congregation that underlies the rest of this book, come along on a quick reconnaissance of a church that most pastors and their teams would agree exhibited a high level of fruitfulness and faithfulness, the early church described in the book of Acts. It is impossible not to be impressed by both the quantity of results— "With many other words he warned them; and he pleaded with them, 'Save yourselves from this corrupt generation.' Those who accepted his message were baptized, and about three thousand were added to their number that day" (2:40-41)—and the quality of results:

> They devoted themselves to the apostles' teaching and to fellowship, to the breaking of bread and to prayer. Everyone was filled with awe at the many wonders and signs performed by the apostles. All the believers were together and had everything in common. They sold property and possessions to give to anyone who had need. Every day they continued to meet together in the temple courts. They broke bread in their homes and ate together with glad and sincere hearts, praising God and enjoying the favor of all the people. And the Lord added to their number daily those who were being saved. (2:42-47)

The Acts of the Apostles presents itself as the second half of a careful investigation of eyewitness testimony concerning the history of Jesus and his disciples. Luke, whose Gospel is the first half, evidently prepared it for intelligent readers like Theophilus who wish to "know the certainty of the things [they] have been taught" (Luke 1:1-4). Acts itself can be viewed in two broad parts, with chapter 13 as a hinge point between them. In terms of the spread of the gospel from Jerusalem to the ends of the earth that the risen Christ spoke of, the first half of the book describes its outworking through Judea and Samaria, while the second half describes its advance through the Greco-Roman world. In terms of leading characters, the first half of the book follows Peter and company, while the second half of the book follows Paul and company. In terms of the development of the church, the first half of Acts traces its growth, while the second half traces its multiplication.

One way of viewing the initial period of expansion presented in chapters 1–12 is to examine a series of summary statements that occur every so often. The first such summary, Acts 2:42-47, appears above. Here are five others:

> They seized Peter and John, and because it was evening, they put them in jail until the next day. But many who heard the message believed, and the number of men grew to about five thousand. (4:3-4 NIV)

> So the word of God spread. The number of disciples in Jerusalem increased rapidly, and a large number of priests became obedient to the faith. (6:7)

> Then the church throughout Judea, Galilee and Samaria enjoyed a time of peace. It was strengthened; and encouraged by the Holy Spirit, it grew in numbers, living in the fear of the Lord. (9:31 NIV)

> The Lord's hand was with them, and a great number of people believed and turned to the Lord. (11:21)

> But the word of God continued to increase and spread. (12:24)

Consider a few essentials that keep showing up in these summary statements. What were the factors that characterized the viral spread of Christianity through the early days of the church? Acknowledging a bias to favor simplicity in making such a list, I suggest these three: the word of God, the Spirit of God, and the mission of God.

Consider three essentials

Without the message of God's grace through Christ, there is no legitimate Christian church. It was Peter's message, echoed by his fellow apostles, that men and women from many nations responded to at Pentecost. The new believers gathered in the temple courts to hear the apostle's teaching; they devoted themselves to it. The growth of the movement is described as the spread of the word. The good news, the gospel, the word of God—without it there is no success, no matter how big the crowd or how impassioned the spirituality. A church cannot win without biblical integrity because without this integrity it ceases to be an authentic church.

As essential as God's truth is to a healthy church, we know from the Scriptures themselves that the letter itself can be treated in a lifeless way. The elite opponents of Jesus were experts in the Scriptures. The Epistle of James indicates that none are more doctrinally correct as the demons of hell. The reason that the word of God is special is that it is of God. The presence of God, the Spirit of God, alive and moving among his people is a *sine qua non* of a victorious church. The summary statements in Acts speak of how everyone was in awe at what God himself was doing in people's lives. The Lord added to his church. The hand of the Lord was with them. Encouraged by the Holy Spirit, the church grew in numbers. A church cannot win without spiritual vitality because without this vitality it ceases to be a living church.

The third critical element, sprinkled through those summary statements in Acts, of the thriving early church movement is the mission of God. Making disciples of all nations exploded on the day of Pentecost and continued to ripple through Jerusalem, Judea, Samaria, and the ends of the earth, just as the risen Christ had announced to those he commissioned. Scan the summary statements in Acts for quantified results of a successful mission: three thousand, then five thousand, followed by rapidly increasing numbers, large numbers, great numbers, daily numbers, continuing to spread. The early church was winning, and the results were posted on the scoreboard of Scripture for us to read through the centuries to follow. Without the urgent purpose of making disciples, of introducing men and women of every tongue and tribe to the Lord of Life, Christians might as well go straight to heaven upon conversion. Everything that believers do on earth, they will do better in heaven and forever, with one exception. In heaven we will never again have the privilege of helping someone else cross the line from death to life in Jesus Christ. We were left here for a reason. A church cannot win without missional accountability because without this accountability it ceases to be an obedient church.

Which is most important?

The word of God, the Spirit of God, and the mission of God—which is most important for the success of the church? Entire ministry movements, institutions, and careers are built emphasizing one over the others. But it is really a trick question, isn't it? If all three are absolutely essential, we cannot afford to lose any of them.

Imagine how inspiring a summary statement in the book of Acts might be if the early church had been missing any one of the three essentials. Let's try an alternate history with no biblical integrity to the Christian movement: "And the disciples were filled with spiritual power and kept making more disciples, and they all believed whatever they wanted to believe." Falls a bit flat, doesn't it? Now let's put the word back in and try a description without spiritual vitality: "And there were more and more disciples learning more and more of the apostles' teaching, and they were exactly the same as they had been before." And now once more, but without mission: "And the disciples worshiped with joy and taught the word with excellence, and when the twelve of them died it was all over."

There is a second reason that asking which of the three is most important turns out to be a trick question: not only are each of the three factors essential, they are also interrelated in such a way that a church cannot truly have any of them without having all of them. For the success or health of a church, these three criteria are more like facets of one gem than like three separate stones. If a church responds properly to any one of the three, it will lead the church to the other two. For example, an authentic submission to the word of God must move a church to seek the very presence of God himself and to obey God in mission—for that is what the word teaches. An authentic willingness to yield to the Spirit of God will propel a church to love God's word and to fulfill his purpose for its activity in the world—for that is what the Spirit desires. And an authentic commitment to the mission of God will drive a church to seek the power of God's Spirit and the content of God's message—for that is what the mission requires.

There are better questions

We are ready to answer the central question of this chapter. What is it that makes a winning church? Churches that are successful, that are healthy, that are pleasing to God and therefore instructive to other churches are those that manifest biblical integrity, spiritual vitality, and missional accountability. They bow to the authority of Scripture, they seek the presence of Christ, and they hold themselves accountable for bearing much fruit.

The thesis of this book is that congregations that are winning—in terms of word, Spirit, and mission—make better decisions than other congregations, better than most congregations, better than typical congregations. To identify this kind of ministry in practical terms, here is the sequence of questions we might ask:

1. Has this congregation been growing numerically?
2. Has its growth included making new disciples?
3. Has this growing, evangelistic congregation been reproducing other congregations?
4. Has this growing, evangelistic, reproducing congregation been advancing mission at a global level?
5. Has this growing, evangelistic, reproducing, globally missional congregation remained faithful to the essential teachings of Scripture?
6. Has this growing, evangelistic, reproducing, globally missional, biblically faithful congregation been seeking the face of God in all that it does?

If we can get a substantial, albeit imperfect affirmative to this sequence of questions, let's deem it a winning church and ask one more question: how does it make decisions? That's what the rest of this book is about.

Where this book is going

Just as sometimes there is a meeting before the meeting, sometimes there is a decision before the decision. People and organizations already have their broadest and deepest assumptions in place long before they formally deliberate on any particular action they might select. Part 1 of this book covers five critical value choices that thriving congregations tend to take in a different direction than most. Getting the big questions right, the values that will shape successful behavior, makes all the difference when it's time to fish or cut bait in ministry.

In Part 2 of the book, we move from values to healthy decision-making behaviors. The devil is in the details they say, but healthy churches chase him out of those details whenever he shows up. Sorting out "who decides what" eliminates much of the confusion and frustration experienced in stagnant churches. There are separate roles for the congregation, staff, lead pastor, board, and tribe. Once those are clarified, we cover a dozen or so typical decisions that most churches face, and talk about best practices in each case. Finally, we catalog a series of top ten decision-process dysfunctions to avoid, related to each of the key players.

There is not enough paper in the world for us to identify every good way to do church and every bad way to do church. However, the combination of values, roles, practices, and pitfalls that we do cover in this book should leave you with a useful sense of what kind of decision-making sets apart the minority of churches that are highly fruitful from the rest.

SUMMARY AND PREVIEW

- *Everybody seems to have a list for what makes a church successful.*

- *The descriptions in Acts of a thriving early church offer insight.*

- *Biblical integrity, spiritual vitality, and missional accountability emerge as three essentials.*

- *It is not helpful to pit one essential against another; the word, Spirit, and mission of God are nonnegotiable and interrelated.*

- *Exceptional congregations that score big on mission—without neglecting the word or the Spirit—make better decisions.*

- Fish or Cut Bait *is organized in two parts: getting the big questions right ahead of time, and getting the devil out of the details.*

The next chapter identifies a handful of overriding considerations that tend to guide the decision making of winning congregations.

PART ONE
FIRST GET THE BIG QUESTIONS RIGHT

CHAPTER ONE

Five Value Choices

It's not hard to make decisions
when you know what your values are.
Roy Disney

THE GERMANS WERE NOT INVITED TO the Olympic Games of 1924 in Paris, the second such snub in a row for having started the last war. The Americans won by far the most medals and the most gold medals, including three in swimming by Johnny Weissmuller, better known as Tarzan in later years. But the most fascinating story from the 1924 Games concerns the "Flying Scotsman," who refused to run on Sunday.

Eric Liddell became a household name after the 1981 movie *Chariots of Fire* portrayed his story and that of his fellow British Olympians. As depicted in the film, Liddell, a devout Christian and son of Scottish missionaries to China, faces a difficult decision. His best personal event is the 100-meter race, but to compete he will have to run in a heat on Sunday and thereby violate his conviction against playing sports on the Lord's Day. In spite of pressure from the British Olympic Committee and the Prince of Wales, among others, Liddell chooses not to compete in the 100 meter. On the day of the race, he is shown watching from the stands. When his friend asks, "Any regrets, Eric? You're not down there with them?" He replies, "Yeah. No doubts though."

Though he was a sprinter and not expected to excel in a longer race, Eric Liddell switches to the 400 meter, which required no running on Sunday. As he sets up on the starting line, he is handed a note that an American fellow believer has written, which reads, "It says in the Good Book, 'He that honors me, I will honor.' Good luck." Liddell wins the gold medal.

Chariots of Fire took some liberties with a few details of the 1924 Games, particularly the timeline. Eric Liddell actually knew the Olympic schedule months in advance and made his hard decision well ahead of sailing for Paris. The essential events, however, are true to history. He did give up his best shot at a gold medal to live by his convictions, and the Prince of Wales and others pressured him to reconsider. And as we all now know, he did bring home the gold against the odds.

Eric Liddell made a difficult, potentially costly, and unpopular decision, but he did so with confidence. Why? Because he had made more fundamental choices years earlier about what was most important to him in life. His values were firmly in place long before the specific decision confronted him. Liddell was in every sense a winner. Churches that win, in God's view of their purpose, likewise make difficult decisions with a courage that flows from value choices previously settled. In this chapter, we will overview five such fundamental choices, each of which is further explored in a chapter of its own.

Big choices make hard choices easier

Church leaders face all kinds of decisions. Some, like which room to use for worship practice, are constant operational decisions that manage week-to-week ministry activities. Some, like which increases and cuts to make in the budget, are regular planning decisions that shape each ministry year. Some, like whether to ask dearly loved but hopelessly divisive Jim to step off the board, are gut-wrenching, urgent decisions that arise through conflict. Still others, like whether to start a third worship service or get a larger building, are occasional strategic decisions that create long-term consequences both intended and unintended. Cutting across all of these categories is the simple spectrum of easy to hard.

There is one more group of decisions, however, that has a profound influence on all the others. This group can be reduced to a single question: *what is important?* Or, even more powerful: *what is more important than the best alternative?* More on this refinement of the question in a moment.

Before going into the five big value choices, there are two pitfalls that should be flagged in the process of identifying congregational values.

The trap of paper values

Publishing a set of core values is a common practice in congregations these days. One need only peruse a custom-printed bulletin cover or an "About Us" website page to find them. Unfortunately, there are at least two major problems that render many such lists under the heading "Our Core Values" nearly useless. The first problem is that the list contains what is supposed to be important instead of what actually *is* important. The second problem is each item on the list is compared either to a contrasting evil or to nothing at all.

With regard to the first problem, consider Main Street Gospel Church, which proclaims "helping people find Christ" as a core value. Sunday after Sunday the congregation sings gospel songs from the era of Moody and Sankey. Regardless of the sermon topic, the preacher winds it up by asking anyone who wants to "get saved today" to walk down the aisle to find out how. The weekly bulletin devotes half a page to news from missionaries the church supports financially. However, as a result of these gospel-related activities, few non-Christians visit Main Street Gospel Church, and those few who do feel that the people there are speaking a strange religious language. This strange language seems to mean a great deal to the members of MSGC but does not help the uninitiated find Christ or even want to find him. It may, in fact, help them want to find the nearest exit.

What's wrong? Is it just a matter of updating to newer church music and language? Would these newcomers be better helped to find Christ if they heard vague phrases about Jesus put to hip-hop tunes and if the preacher—no, the "spiritual director"—said, "Give God a clap offering"? Or is the problem deeper?

What Main Street Gospel Church states as a "core value" is not what MSGC treats as important in terms of its behavior. The official list says the value is *helping people find Christ*. The real value is *helping people who have already found Christ feel good about it and sending money overseas to those who (hopefully) are helping people find Christ*. If Main Street Gospel Church actually valued helping people find Christ, it might review its language to see that it is based not on whether it contains the shibboleths of our ecclesiastical tribe but on whether it clearly and graciously explains who Christ is and how to know him personally. It might review its music not for its age or style but for how it makes guests feel about the message that it conveys.

So the first problem for a congregation to avoid, in the process of identifying its fundamental values, is simply composing an attractive list of what we might call "official values" without thinking through the changes in behavior that such statements would require to be worth the paper on which they are printed. **If we will not give up real money, real time, and real comfort for something, then it is not a real value for us.**

The trap of values in a vacuum

The second problem to avoid regarding core values is failing to rank them against their most meaningful alternatives. This problem frequently shows up through a list of undeniably good things that are not compared to anything else. For example, if you were looking for a new church home, you might do an Internet search and then go to the website of a likely possibility. Under a tab labeled "Our Values" you could find the following statement:

At Community Christian Chapel we value . . .

- *The Bible*
- *The Holy Spirit*
- *Jesus Christ*
- *Prayer*
- *Love*
- *Faith*

The list might be shorter or longer, but you get the idea. Would you be able to choose for or against joining Community Christian Chapel based on this list? Do you think the leaders of CCC would be able to choose for or against, say, building a new educational wing based on this list? One reason that such a list may prove sterile when it comes to decision making is that each item, while good in itself, hangs in midair with no point of contrast.

Would the following revision provide more guidance?

At Community Christian Chapel we value . . .

- *The Bible, not error*
- *The Holy Spirit, not the devil*
- *Jesus Christ, not idols*
- *Prayer, not cursing*
- *Love, not hate*
- *Faith, not unbelief*

Probably not. When you rank something good against something bad, it is obvious that the good thing is better. To make a value choice in a way that can guide real decisions in a challenging world, it is much more useful to rank the item against its best alternative, or we might say, its most likely competing value. Good must be ranked beside good in order for us to make a choice about which good thing carries more weight. No one wants to make a bad decision. What individuals face and what congregations face is choosing one good over the other.

Eric Liddell loved to run. It was good. He also loved doing what he thought would please his Lord—another good thing. Which did he love more? Did the ranking of one good thing against another good thing help him make tricky decisions? You bet. (Just don't place that bet on a Sunday.)

In the same way, when a congregation makes its big value choices by thinking through their most meaningful competing values, it can develop a set of priorities that provide powerful guidance for its decision making. For example, let's say the leaders at Cathedral of Truth adopt the following value and determine to live by it: *sharing God's love with others is more important than speaking against the sins of society.* The folk at CT think that sharing God's love is good. They also think that speaking against sin is good. They intend to do all the good they can. But they have decided that, on the whole, sharing God's love is more important.

So one day the pastor at Cathedral of Truth, which maintains an outreach to young men and women caught up in the sex trade, finds a piece of mail on his desk. It is a personal letter from a fellow pastor in town asking to recruit the CT congregation for a protest march on the local adult bookstore. The pastor reflects on the core values of CT (or more likely doesn't, because they are a part of him) and takes the following three actions: (1) He tosses the letter in the wastebasket. (2) He phones his pastor friend to decline the request but to offer CT's child daycare service free to participants in the march. (3) He drafts an e-mail to the woman who owns the adult bookstore stating that, while he agrees with the position of those marching, he would prefer to express his convictions through respectful dialogue if she would be open to that.

The kind of wording in CT's value statement may make you feel uncomfortable. Perhaps you would give the greater weight to the good of confronting sin. That's between you and God. Or perhaps you don't agree with the example. That is not the point right now. What makes the statement seem biting, whichever good alternative you prioritize and whatever example you would offer, is that the words have teeth. Most of the core values we have seen leave no bite marks on any practical decision because they are toothless. Something to chew on.

Introducing the big five questions

Just what are the key value questions that a congregation must answer if it is to be effective in its decision making? Doubtless there are any number of ways to organize these priorities. In order to highlight the distinction of churches that thrive from churches that don't, there are five major questions explored in the next several chapters.

1. What must be done?
2. Who says so?
3. Who takes the lead?
4. What's it going to cost?
5. What if there's trouble?

The **first question** raises the issue of mission and vision. By *mission* I mean the enduring and universal imperative for the church. By *vision* I mean the time-limited and unique imperative for a particular congregation. There are many things that could be done and even should be done by the church. But what is it that must be done? What will be the driving force? The *raison d'être*? The *sine qua non*? The reason to get out of bed in the morning?

The **second question** is one of authority. If the controlling imperative of the first question is challenged, who gets to decide the right answer? By way of analogy, the sixteenth-century Reformation is said to have turned on two overarching principles: *Sola Fidei*, or salvation through faith alone, and *Sola Scriptura*, the final authority of Scripture alone. The first of these is called the *material principle* of the Reformation; the second is called the *formal principle* of the Reformation. The material principle answered the question, How can we become children of God? Luther's answer was, "Through faith alone." The formal principle answered the question, How can we know how we can become children of God? According to Luther, "On the authority of Scripture alone." The first two questions of the big five above concern a different subject but bear a similar relationship to each other.

The **third question** relates to leadership. Is the congregation expected to rise up spontaneously and fulfill its purpose *en masse* without human direction? Do we look to the pastor to take the initiative? What about a board or council? What about the paid or volunteer staff? Bottom line:

where do we look for primary leadership in order to accomplish the mission? Without a clear answer, congregations suffer nothing but conflict and confusion.

The **fourth question** is tactical in nature. How should resources be managed in order to accomplish the mission? What is it going to take to succeed? Are we willing to pay that cost?

Question number five addresses the active opposition and passive resistance that inevitably form against leadership on a mission. What is most important when conflict arises?

Each of the big five is critical in and of itself. All of the five, however, are related to one another. Logically, we might do well to reverse the order of the first two questions and make the last two questions parallel. Follow the relationships in the diagram below:

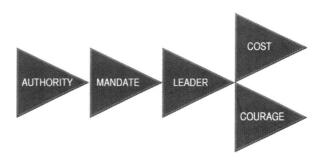

Someone has the legitimate right (authority) to determine what the church must do (mandate). Then someone must mobilize the church to do it (leader), both allocating resources (cost) and overcoming opposition (courage). The answers to these five value questions that are chosen by highly fruitful congregations differ remarkably from the majority. And these distinctive answers guide those congregations through the blizzard of decisions they encounter on their journey. The chapters that follow will deal with the big five questions in the intuitive order in which they might best be asked: What must be done? Who says so? Who takes the lead? What's it going to cost? What if there's trouble?

One final note about Eric Liddell. His courage of conviction in 1924 was not a unique flash of nobility. It was, rather, a typical display of his character. After the Olympics he returned to China and served as a missionary from 1925 to 1943, when he was imprisoned in a Japanese internment camp in occupied China. He died in the camp in February 1945, five months before it was liberated. In 2008, the year of the Beijing Olympics, the Chinese government revealed that during a prisoner exchange approved by Winston Churchill, Liddell turned down a chance for release from the prison camp and gave his place to a pregnant woman. Even his own family members were unaware of this sacrifice. Knowing his values, however, would they have been surprised?

SUMMARY AND PREVIEW

- *Big choices at the value level shape all the decisions that follow.*

- *Values with meaning give more weight to one good than to another.*

- *Pitfalls to avoid include values without comparison and comparison only to something negative.*

- *The most powerful way to construct value statements is to rank the good alongside its nearest competing good.*

- *The big five questions are: What must be done? Who says so? Who takes the lead? What's this going to cost? and What if there's trouble?*

- *Winning churches make different choices from other churches on the five questions of authority, mandate, leadership, cost, and courage.*

The next chapter tackles the first of the big five questions in their intuitive order: what must be done?

CHAPTER TWO

What Must Be Done?

We all want progress, but if you're on the wrong road,
progress means doing an about-turn and walking back to the right road;
in that case, the man who turns back soonest is the most progressive.
C. S. Lewis

THE 2001 UNITED STATES PRESIDENTIAL inauguration was unique for several reasons. One was simply that it marked the first such transfer of power in the twenty-first century and the new millennium. Another was that it followed one of the most contentious disputes over election results in American history, a dispute that required a Supreme Court decision to resolve. A third distinction was that the new president, George W. Bush, was the son of a former president who bore the same first and last name—this being noteworthy but actually not unique because it had happened once before, almost two hundred years earlier with the John Adamses. And then there was the matter of the Westport Wildcats.

High school marching bands in the United States shine for their classmates in football halftime shows, for their parents in parades, and for each other in band competitions. On occasion they have the opportunity to showcase their talent at a high-profile televised event. As the story goes, Westport High School, in a small New England community, received an invitation for its band to perform at the presidential inauguration in Washington, D.C. What an honor! They declined.

Why would a small-town band turn down the chance to play on a national stage? Because the band at Westport High School was a marching band but they were being asked to sit and perform as a concert band. What the news media couldn't believe was that the students would forfeit the once-in-a-lifetime invitation. The director replied, "Sorry. That

27

is not what we are about. We are about being a precision marching band, and we will not be distracted. We will not allow ourselves to get pulled away from our single focus."

When it comes to making difficult choices, whether as a marching band or a local church, it is important to know the reason you exist: what *must* be done?

Good decisions are driven by mission

Although Jesus gave many instructions and examples to his followers over the course of his ministry before the Crucifixion, none are as explicitly presented as the now familiar words at the end of the first Gospel: "Then Jesus came to them and said, 'All authority in heaven and on earth has been given to me. Therefore go and make disciples of all nations, baptizing them in the name of the Father and of the Son and of the Holy Spirit, and teaching them to obey everything I have commanded you. And surely I am with you always, to the very end of the age'" (Matt. 28:18-20).

While three important participles qualify the command, there is a single imperative: to make new learners (*mathetes*) from every culture (*ethne*). *Going* is how we find them, *baptizing* is how we mark them, and *teaching* them to obey is how we mature them; but the core of the mission is to *make more of them*. The good news is too good to keep to ourselves.

Mission, which belongs to the whole church, is implemented in each individual congregation by means of vision, which is a picture of what mission accomplished would look like in a particular place and time. In his insightful and analytical book *Pursuing the Full Kingdom Potential of Your Congregation*, George Bullard depicts the relationship of vision in a thriving ministry to three other variables: relationships, programs, and management.

> Imagine a car as a metaphor for a congregation. Place Vision, Relationships, Programs, and Management in this vehicle in the seat best suited for each to symbolize a faithful, effective, and innovative journey for a congregation. Who would drive? Vision, of course. Vision would be driving and fueling the forward progress of the vehicle. Who would navigate? Relationships would navigate and flavor the quality of the journey.

Who would be in the back seat behind Relationships? Programs would sit behind Relationships in a supporting role. It would provide the programs, ministries, and activities through which the best possible relationships could happen with God, with one another, and with the context the congregation serves.

So, Management would be in the back seat behind Vision? Yes. It would provide the administrative infrastructure that allows Vision to engage in *"FaithSoaring"* in response to God's leadership.[1]

To extend Bullard's metaphor for decision making, consider the basic question that Vision would be asking from behind the steering wheel when faced with a fork in the road. Since Vision is concerned with the intended destination, it would ask, "Which road will take us to where we want to wind up?" But what about a congregation that has lost its primacy of mission and clarity of vision? Who winds up driving the car? Management does, according to Bullard. And once again, to build on his car story for our decision-making topic, what is the question that Management would be asking from the driver's seat at the same fork in the road?

Management is concerned with controlling costs and risks so it would ask, "Which is the better road?" This is certainly a valid question, but one that must be kept subordinate to the larger mission.

If management becomes dominant over vision in the critical choices of a ministry, the ride may be smooth but on a downhill-glide path. In Bullard's words, "The longer Management drives and the longer Vision sleeps, the more likely the congregation will engage in activities that cause it to age and become more passive and less vital. The long-term result of this pattern is death."[2] The congregation that thrives and pleases its Lord is one that makes his heart for making new disciples, rather than internal issues, the driving force behind critical choices.

Cracking into the neighborhood

When Dr. Clive Neil arrived as pastor of Bedford Central Presbyterian Church, he found that it was disconnected and no longer in service—not the telephone but the ministry. This historic congregation in Brooklyn, New York, had changed with its neighborhood from white to black over the years except for two key factors. One was leadership. Dr. Neil, a Caribbean American, would be Bedford Central's first black pastor. The other was community engagement. Much of the congregation commuted in to church without touching the neighborhood.

Because he believed the mission of Christ must drive the ministry of the congregation, Dr. Neil knew he had to reorient his church from inward to outward in its focus. This transformation required three steps. The first step was to gain credibility with his flock by building relationships over the first eighteen months. The second step was to train leaders who could become his allies. The third step was convincing a skeptical neighborhood that the congregation was serious about its commitment to blessing the people who lived nearby.

The greatest oppression in the community was crime stemming from the drug trade. Pastor Neil and his people joined with locals to shut down the two crack houses in the neighborhood. After that, the community realized the congregation didn't just drive in for the show anymore; they showed up where it counted. Over the years since that breakthrough, worship attendance has grown from 80 to 600, and four other congregations are led by lay pastors trained and supported by Bedford Central Presbyterian Church.

Off the wall is on the mark

Whereas vision rather than management tends to dominate new churches because of the necessities of the start-up years, so it is also with the more effective churches with histories behind them. These churches often take greater intentionality.

Inwardly focused congregations get hung up on everything from budgets to band instruments. They might even argue about what color to paint the auditorium. Not at Louis Bourque's church. In a municipal region just north of Montreal, Quebec, Église Baptiste Évangélique de Terrebonne-Mascouche is one of the largest evangelical churches in Francophone Canada, with more than five hundred in worship attendance, and it is constantly giving people and dollars away to plant daughter congregations. So what did they do about painting the auditorium? They filled the whole wall with a map of the ten nearby communities where they are starting new churches over a ten-year period. You walk in the place and quickly learn that they take the importance of vision literally.

Louis is a tall Quebecer with broad shoulders, an infectious smile, and a ready bear hug. But if you are an Anglophone, an English-speaking person, you might not have wanted to cross his path a few decades ago. As an unbeliever he lived in Quebec and was an angry young separatist with drug issues during the violent 1970s. Today as *pasteur principal* at Terrebonne-Mascouche, Louis loves *la belle province* more than ever, but he weeps over it in prayer instead of lashing out in anger. He still wants to take over the whole province, but only on behalf of the kingdom of God. As of this writing his people have planted half of those ten churches in their vision. Any chance of them getting off track and failing to finish? Not as long as Louis can buy paint.

You shape the building, then it shapes you

Wooddale Church near Minneapolis was planning its major facility development at a time when many cutting-edge congregations were opting for buildings that bore no resemblance to a church structure. Millions of dollars was a lot of money to spend on bricks and mortar, so Leith Anderson and his team wanted to get the architecture right.

Going with the nondescript trend would be no better than falling back to red bricks and white columns if it didn't help Wooddale reach the particular nonchurchgoers of their ministry area. What type of campus would be most attractive to their target community? How could they know in advance? Well, they asked.

It so happens that the Twin Cities are filled with ex-Catholics and ex-Lutherans who never go to church but who would want a church to "look like a church" if they ever did. The mission shaped the building. Outside, from the highway, Wooddale's striking facility is a modern structure with a styling inspired by the arches and spires of a classic cathedral. Inside, the best features of hotel lobbies, schools, civic centers, and restaurants help people feel comfortable with where to go and what to do. The learning point, of course, is not for other churches to mimic Wooddale's architecture but to apply Wooddale's priority on mission. Cost is important, theology plays a role, and donor preferences carry some weight, but mission must drive the critical choices.

One more thing about Wooddale's mission-driven facility has nothing to do with its architecture. They adopted a policy that all kinds of community groups could use their facilities for all kinds of events and programs—the National Multiple Sclerosis Society, Alcoholics Anonymous, Al-Anon, Gambler's Anonymous, and others. But there is one kind of outside group that is not allowed to use the church campus—Christian organizations. Why? Because Leith's team wants the nonchurchgoing people and leaders of the community to be in and out of the place all the time and to think of it as a normal place to be. And when the time comes that some of them do want to seek out a church, they already have one where they've been many times, even if not for a worship service.

Sometimes you can't afford to keep the money

Mission drives reproduction, not just expansion, of thriving churches. Richmond Emmanuel Church on Canada's Pacific coast faced the decision under Silas Ng's leadership of whether to plant a new Anglican church for Chinese Canadians across the country from them in Toronto. The Richmond congregation, while experiencing solid conversion growth, did not own property and had only recently moved into a larger and much more costly rented facility. Nevertheless, despite the challenges of their own increasing needs and a difficult economy, Richmond Emmanuel chose to plant the new congregation under the leadership of Rev. Edmund Ho in 2009. The church plant, Toronto Emmanuel, grew from eight original team members to forty and baptized ten new believers in the first year. Incredibly, among those who joined with the small but fruitful new congregation was a man who had waited ten years for just such a ministry, to which he would donate six acres of prime real estate in Greater Toronto. The result is a $150 million project under way to include facilities for Toronto Emmanuel Church, a community center, and five hundred condominiums for seniors. The leaders at Richmond Emmanuel had counted the cost and moved prayerfully and cautiously with the decision to launch a daughter church. However, they made the decision based not on convenience but on their mission to be a disciple-making church that reproduced others of like mind. Bishop Ng had no way of knowing how God had ten years earlier prepared an outpouring of his provision for the occasion.

Know when to hold 'em; know when to fold 'em

Mission over management drove Flipside Christian Church, under Karl Roth's leadership, in its multiplication efforts, with two very different outcomes. Flipside was a new church plant itself, but one that started with a commitment to reproducing after its own kind early and often. In fewer than ten years since its own inception, Flipside has launched two additional campuses. One was started in a large retirement community. The other was aimed at the ragged edge of society and named Flipside 13 after its original location, The Lucky 13, a heavy metal bar in Fresno. In both cases, the mission to reach all kinds of people drove the decisions to start the new works. How did things go? Both grew well in terms of nickels and noses. Within three years, Flipside 13 was released as a freestanding, self-supporting local church, relocated inside a center city mall. The other daughter congregation, in the retirement community, also grew— to more than one hundred in attendance—but after just a few years Flipside closed it down. Why? Who in their right mind closes down a new congregation that is growing and that is already larger than the average-sized church in the United States (that is, 75 members)? In all of its growth, the people had not reached one person for Christ. Karl Roth and his team are not into numbers for the sake of numbers; they are committed to increasing the number of new disciples so that the kingdom of God expands. So what would look like success to others was a sign to redeploy their energies in a more fruitful direction.

Winning churches value wise management but they don't let it take the wheel of the car. Mission drives because the destination is more important than the road. Steer around the potholes whenever possible, but don't choose a smooth, wide boulevard to nowhere.

SUMMARY AND PREVIEW

- *Congregations that win long term aim to make decisions that please Christ as the Lord and Head of the church, the One who owns it and authorizes its legitimate purpose.*

- *Mission drives the agenda of winning congregations, constantly turning them outward to those who don't yet have a relationship with Christ and his people.*

- *Outward mission can be criticized by the Christians within.*

- *Putting mission first shapes buildings and their use.*

- *Bold risks accompany a priority on mission.*

- *Sometimes mission means closing down a ministry first.*

Not everyone agrees that making new disciples should be the reason a congregation exists. The next chapter grapples with the question of whose agenda to follow: who says so?

CHAPTER THREE

Who Says So?

God has editing rights over our prayers.
He will . . . edit them, correct them,
bring them in line with His will and
then hand them back to us to be resubmitted.
Stephen Crotts

THE DIET OF WORMS WAS A MESS. Martin Luther appeared as ordered before Charles V and other secular authorities. The pope had already excommunicated him three months earlier in January of 1520; now the emperor was deciding whether to execute him as well. You could get yourself into a lot of trouble in those days for saying that God could not be bought off with cash. Fortunately, Luther's local prince, Frederick the Wise, had negotiated a safe conduct for the renegade preacher both to and from the Diet. It was the "from" part that would come in handy.

Luther's revulsion at the practice of selling indulgences led him to ask a big question: since buying your way into heaven couldn't be right, just how could a person obtain the forgiveness of sins? After years of studying and teaching the New Testament at the University of Wittenberg, he came to this answer: salvation came by grace alone, through faith alone. It was the gift of God, paid in full by the blood of Christ. In the city of Worms, Luther was forced to address a follow-up question: who says so? For that one, Luther cast himself on the Scriptures rather than on the bishop of Rome: "My conscience is captive to the Word of God. I cannot and will not recant anything, since it is neither safe nor right to go against conscience. May God help me. Amen."

When a congregation answers the big question of what must be done with the mission of making new disciples, not everyone is going to like that answer. For this reason, a missional congregation will need an answer to the authority question: who says so?

Good decisions aim to please Christ

Congregations that thrive over the long term make formative choices springing from a settled conviction that the church belongs not to its members or to its movement but to its Head, the Lord Jesus Christ. Most any Christian congregation would profess this belief as its own. What separates the winners from the windbags is whether a congregation's future-shaping choices reflect a serious effort to discern and execute the agenda of Christ for a church that, after all, belongs to him in the first place.

As simple as it sounds, no other consideration for making decisions runs as deep as the question of who owns the church. Every significant choice will alter the future in way that will please some and displease others among the stakeholders. So whom should we please? Who has the right to be pleased? Whose church is it, anyway?

When the leaders and influencers in a congregation lose sight of its Owner, it is possible for them to do good, to work hard, to withstand difficulties, to confront evil, to insist on sound teaching, and yet to forsake their love for the One who loved them first and bought them with his own blood. That is precisely the indictment of the church in Ephesus by Christ in the book of Revelation: "I know your deeds, your hard work and your perseverance. I know that you cannot tolerate wicked men, that you have tested those who claim to be apostles but are not, and have found them false. You have persevered and have endured hardships for my name, and have not grown weary. Yet I hold this against you: You have forsaken your first love" (Rev. 2:2-4 NIV).

The record is silent on whether this ministry was growing numerically at the time of this evaluation, in the late first century, but the references to it in the book of Acts and in the Epistle to the Ephesians make clear that the church in that city was the flagship of the Christian movement in Asia Minor, blessed with multiple leaders. When the Apostle Paul departed the province for the last time, he called together those leaders—whom the writer of Acts described as elders (*presbuteros*) and whom Paul addressed as supervisors (*episkopos*) and pastors (*poimen*)—to give them the following charge:

> Keep watch over yourselves and all the flock of which the Holy Spirit has made you overseers. Be shepherds of the church of God, which he bought with his own blood. I know that after I leave, savage wolves will come in among you and will not spare the flock. Even from your own number men will arise and distort the truth in order to draw away disciples after them. So be on your guard! Remember that for three years I never stopped warning each of you night and day with tears. (Acts 20:28-31 NIV)

Judging from the message to the Ephesian church decades later in the book of Revelation, apparently these leaders were faithful and effective in terms of guarding their extensive flock from error. They did what Paul asked them to do and kept doing it for many years. The Ephesians were, however, unfaithful in another sense—the sense in which wives and husbands are to be faithful to each other. They fell out of love with Christ. They lost the underlying relationship that seeps through the wording of Paul's original exhortation to them. The leaders were to serve a church that Jesus had "bought with his own blood." Paul himself had for three years labored in this precious church "night and day with tears." It would seem that sometime between the mid-60s and the mid-90s of the first century, although the sweat kept flowing in the Ephesian church, the tears dried up. They kept the faith but lost the love.

What's in a name?

Keeping Christ and his agenda for the church at the center makes all the difference for good decisions, and believers recognize it when they see it. A large historic congregation in southern California had once been hung up on the pride of their name and the stature that it represented in the community. Being known as "First Baptist Church" had come to

mean more than humbly living and sharing the love of God with others. Efforts at renewal, which included an initiative to change the name of the congregation, met with resistance. Then the leaders creatively proposed a new name that the old guard had trouble opposing, a name that showcased the core issue of ownership with the simple addition of a single word. The sign now reads "Christ First Baptist Church." Gulp.

In business, the managers have a responsibility to protect the interests and to carry out the directives of the owner or owners of the enterprise. Public corporations have shareholders. Private companies have a sole proprietor or a set of partners. A Christian congregation is not a business; and though it may be incorporated, it does not have shareholders. It does, however, have an Owner. Regardless of its legal status and regardless of its ecclesiastical polity, a congregation legitimately belongs only to its Lord and Head, Jesus Christ.

Christ is the Owner of the church, the One whose interests are at stake. Alternatives to pleasing Christ include people pleasing, crowd pleasing, pastor pleasing, donor pleasing, culture pleasing, and emotional-terrorist pleasing. Not all of these pleasings are inherently bad—except for that last one—but they must not compete with pleasing the Owner.

Sometimes your knees knock

Pleasing Christ includes both knowing his will and doing it. Early in his pastoral career, Leith Anderson, senior pastor of Wooddale Church near Minneapolis, discerned that the biggest obstacle to God's purposes in his congregation at that particular time was a lack of evangelism. What was worse was that he was no good at it, and neither was anyone else in the church. Nevertheless, he was absolutely convinced that cracking the door open on bringing people to Christ was the next big thing that needed to happen. This did not come from his preferences or those of his flock. It came from a conviction that it was what Christ wanted.

Driven by that overriding consideration, to please Christ, Leith read a book called *Evangelism Explosion* (EE) by D. James Kennedy and started visiting the homes of people who visited the church. Though he was a pastor, he felt awkward and artificial at every step. At first, he actually felt ill after getting back to his car. Not surprisingly, he had no results. Finally, after many weeks of barren efforts, someone shocked him by saying that yes, they would like him to explain to them how to receive Christ. Since Leith had never gotten that far in the presentation before, he had to ask them to meet again later, so he could refresh his memory on that part of the EE presentation. In the end, a trickle of new believers began to come into the church. By his own assessment, Leith never became a gifted personal evangelist; but God honored his obedience and sent others onto the team with those gifts. Some of those believers had even come to faith through those early, stumbling efforts—efforts aimed at pleasing the Owner of the congregation.[1]

If you must predict, predict often

In California's Central Valley, two sponsoring churches joined forces to establish a flagship church in Madera County under the auspices of

GHC Network. An innovative new housing development, Rio Mesa, was planned, and the opportunity to reach the people who would move into it seemed ideal. Karl Roth and his wife, Shellie, accepted the challenge, raised significant funding, and recruited a strong ministry team.

The good news was that Flipside Christian Church launched with a high birth weight and began to reach residents of the existing communities in the area. The bad news was that the promised housing development never materialized, so the strategy had to be revised. The two parent churches wanted to see Flipside target North Fresno, but Karl and his team still believed that God had called him to reach the Madera side of the San Joaquin River, even if Rio Mesa was not going to materialize. And so, with some anxiety and criticism, the new church relocated to the high school campus in the small town of Madera Ranchos. Flipside now has a major influence in a community of eighteen hundred residents as a church of five hundred members that is planting daughter churches in the region. Seeking to follow Christ, even through unexpected circumstances and pressures, is the overriding concern for critical decisions in a winning church.

Integrity calls for courage

Bishop Silas Ng, rector of Richmond Emmanuel Church in Greater Vancouver, British Columbia, once faced a difficult issue of conscience in his ministry. Originally from Hong Kong, he had come to Vancouver and accepted the challenge of planting a new congregation to reach the growing Chinese Canadian community. Within three and a half years the congregation was self-supporting, with two hundred in attendance, including ninety-one adults either baptized or confirmed as new Christians during that period. As an Anglican, Rev. Ng was committed to serve under authority and did so with joy. When his denominational hierarchy violated his conscience before Christ, however, on a matter of sexual morality, he and his fledgling congregation made the difficult choice to break ties with the mainline denomination in Canada.

Consistent with their value on connectional ministry and apostolic succession, they did not become independent but rather placed themselves under the Anglican Mission in the Americas under the authority of the Primate of Rwanda, Archbishop Emmanuel Kolini.

Rev. Ng did not wish to be rebellious in any way, only to be fully submissive to the one Lord of the church and to fellow servants with the same desire within the Worldwide Anglican Communion. In the decade that followed, Silas Ng was selected as bishop over the sixteen AMiA parishes that comprise the Anglican Coalition in Canada. Rick Warren spoke at his consecration service. Bishop Ng's own congregation near Vancouver has become a large and influential one, still growing through evangelism in three language groups—Cantonese, Mandarin, and English. They know Who owns the church.

To please the Owner, find out what he wants

The word and prayer are indispensable channels for knowing what will please the Lord, if that is in fact the priority of a church. For that reason they should be better tied to key decisions. How often does an emotional influencer shift the direction of a decision by passionately declaring "what God is saying to us right now" without any pause in the momentum of persuasion for the group to pray and ask for guidance? How often does a church force out a pastor under criticism without ever opening the New Testament during a board meeting, reading the passage about entertaining accusations against an elder,[2] and discussing what kind of process would please the Head of the church? He left some instructions! What good is an official commitment to the authority of Scripture if it is not explicitly applied to big decisions? What good are passionate words about following the Spirit of Christ if he is not actually consulted?

What is more basic to Christianity than its most primitive statement of faith: Jesus is Lord? The winning congregation is one that aims to please him above all others. Therefore, the first and most foundational consideration for making good decisions is to choose whatever course of

FISH OR CUT BAIT

action best pleases Christ according to our best understanding of his directives.

SUMMARY AND PREVIEW

- *Congregations that win long term aim to make decisions that please Christ as the Lord and Head of the church, the One who owns it and authorizes its legitimate purpose.*

- *It's hard to argue with putting Christ first.*

- *Obedience may call us out of our comfort zone.*

- *Following where Christ leads requires changes to our plans.*

- *Honoring Christ requires courageous integrity.*

- *To please Christ means searching his word to learn what he wants.*

The next chapter deals with the big question of how to get started with the mission of Christ: who takes the lead?

CHAPTER FOUR

Who Takes the Lead?

In the building practices of ancient Rome, when scaffolding was removed
from a completed Roman arch, the Roman engineer stood beneath.
If the arch came crashing down, he was the first to know.
Thus his concern for the quality of the arch was intensely personal,
and it is not surprising that so many Roman arches have survived.
Paul Rosenstein-Rodan

BEFORE SERVING AS U.S. AMBASSADOR TO the USSR from 1979 to 1981, Thomas Watson Jr. distinguished himself as a world-class leader at IBM. He took over the reins of International Business Machines from his father, becoming CEO in 1956. Thomas Sr. had already built the company into the industry leader in machines for processing information. That early success had been based on electromechanical technology such as the typewriter, the adding machine, and the punch card. The vision and foresight of the younger Watson recognized that the future lay with the emerging technology of electronics. He took IBM from gears and switches to vacuum tubes and transistors. He took it from 72,500 employees with $892 million in sales in 1956 to 270,000 employees with $8.3 billion in sales in 1971.

Watson not only exhibited strong leadership, however; he valued and developed it in others. On one occasion a junior executive at Big Blue was called into Watson's office after losing the company millions of dollars through a series of poor judgment calls.

"I suppose after that set of mistakes you will want to fire me," said the executive.

"Not at all, young man," replied Watson, "we have just spent a couple of million dollars educating you."[1]

Organizations require leadership. Good organizations require good leadership. Great organizations require great leadership. Great churches understand that concept and place a high value on supporting their lead pastor.

Good decisions support the pastor's leadership

We have already addressed the first two of the five big decisions. (1) What must be done? The mission—to make disciples. That is a higher value than other good and needful tasks such as member care, program quality, and management structure. (2) Who says so? The Lord Jesus Christ, who owns the church and has all authority in heaven and on earth. Influential members of the congregation, whether by personality or power, should be heard and considered but should not be allowed to divert the church from its God-given mission. All right then, that much is settled. We know what must be done. We also know how we know that. And now we just look around the room at each other.

There is an anonymous little story about four people named Everybody, Somebody, Anybody, and Nobody.

> There was an important job to be done and Everybody was sure that Somebody would do it. Anybody could have done it, but Nobody did it. Somebody got angry about that because it was Everybody's job. Everybody thought that Anybody could do it, but Nobody realized that Everybody wouldn't do it. It ended up that Everybody blamed Somebody when Nobody did what Anybody could have done.

This old story is typically used to bemoan a general lack of responsibility, as if everyone should spontaneously stand up and get started on the task at hand. That, however, is not the way life works. In reality, if some significant group mission gets done, it is always a Somebody who takes the initiative to get Everybody moving. That Somebody is the leader.

There is no question that everyone in the body of Christ has been gifted and called to be a minister—that is, a servant. There is no question that teams and groups of leaders are needed to join in common cause under the lordship of Christ and the impetus of the Spirit to get things done and to bear much fruit. It is to be done together in community. Without an effective lead pastor, however, it is simply not going to happen—at least not at your church.

I have never seen a winning church, one that others seek out in order to learn how it's done, that was not guided to that level of healthy growth by a strong lead pastor. Don't misunderstand. There are examples of larger churches with a lack of primary leadership at the top whether by absence, incompetence, or displacement by a group (e.g., board or staff team). But in every one of those cases there has been a lead pastor at some point in the not-too-distant past who led them so effectively that the momentum created then is still having a positive impact—for a while.

What gets in the way of strong leadership?

If the best churches know that the answer to big question number three, Who takes the lead? is the pastor, what is it that gets in the way of other congregations valuing and supporting strong pastoral leadership? And what is the nearest competing value to a value on a strong lead pastor?

With regard to obstacles, there are several. The one at the root is lack of trust. Larger churches tend to become large in part through developing a culture of trust in their pastor. The pastor is expected to be what Lyle Schaller calls "the initiating leader" or "the chief of the tribe." Smaller churches or larger ones that have stopped growing tend to stay that way or decline in part through developing a culture of distrust in their pastor. The pastor is expected to be something called a "spiritual leader," or in Schaller's terminology, "the medicine man of the tribe."[2] Trust or credibility is a commodity that to some degree can be earned, borrowed, lent, or granted. One of the best treatments concerning the lead pastor's earning and usage of trust is an article by Leith Anderson about what he calls

"Parish Poker."[3] The culture and systems in a church, however, also have a great deal to do with whether what we might call the "trust economy" in a congregation is conducive to the earning of trust. When people prefer to talk more about checks and balances than about risks and rewards, the pastor may be trying to raise a crop of trust in a dry and thirsty land.

Some obstacles to building trust in strong lead pastors are the fault of the pastor. These include false humility, denial, people pleasing, and, of course, moral failure. False humility, unlike true humility, fails to recognize the value of the good gifts that God has given to leaders for the benefit of his church. The Apostle Paul has the right perspective as he writes, "By the grace God has given me, I laid a foundation as a wise builder, and someone else is building on it. But each one should build with care" (1 Cor. 3:10). He is not shy about referring to himself as an expert architect, but he acknowledges it as a gift of God's grace. Pastors who are overly self-deprecating undercut their own legitimate authority and credibility, and worse, they do so for the next pastor as well.

Some pastors are strong leaders but find it useful to deny it publicly. Many years ago I heard the high-profile pastor of one of the largest churches in the United States try to convince the pastors attending his conference that he was just one of the fifty elders at his church, except that he happened to be the "pastor-teacher." The reality was that thirty-seven of the fifty elders on his board were his staff pastors. That power and the national following of his radio program gave him more than enough clout to run the church as he liked. Unfortunately, instead of teaching young pastors how to use authority responsibly to serve others, he denied that he had any. Such denial teaches the wrong lesson. If it is so important to deny strong leadership, it must be something bad. That only reinforces a culture of control in dysfunctional congregations.

People pleasing is yet another obstacle to building trust. Almost ten years ago I heard Randy Frazee, who went on to become a teaching pastor at Willow Creek with Bill Hybels, say to a small group of mentoring pastors, "You cannot choose whether or not there will be pain in your

ministry. You can, however, choose from whom the pain will come." A pastor who stands strong and presses forward for mission will encounter flack, and some of it will hurt. Even people claiming to be your closest friends may undercut you when you need their support the most. However, a pastor who gives in to every influencer in the congregation to keep as many people happy as possible will also experience pain, simply because the self-focus of various individuals will conflict. The difference is that one source of pain makes the pain worthwhile. Pain that comes from self-protection isn't worth it. Better to move forward with those who want to move forward.

Moral failure is the most obvious killer of credibility a pastor can unleash. Whether the issue is sex or money, the pastor who crosses certain lines will never regain all of what a scandal destroys, even when repentance, forgiveness, and rehabilitation is all it can be. Despite the fact that some pastors blow it in major ways, it is a self-defeating church that creates a structure and culture designed to protect a congregation from the influence of a bad pastor. A healthy culture and structure identifies and removes such a pastor instead, then calls a pastor it can trust and follow.

The nearest competing value

For a larger, growing church, the nearest competing value to a strong lead pastor who takes the lead tends to be influential board members. This requires some explanation.

A healthy, missional, growing congregation of five hundred people or more is not likely to be drawn off track by power players at the congregational level. That kind of challenge to pastoral leadership is characteristic of smaller churches and is one of the things that keeps them small. Once a church breaks well beyond the infamous two hundred barrier and the next barrier, around four hundred, any erosion of the pastor's leadership is likely to come from within the board. Not by the board itself, mind you, but by one or another of its members. Just as the congregation is a group, the board is a group—and groups do not lead; they are led. If someone says, "The congregation feels this way," you can be sure that it is the agenda of an individual influencer and his or her friends you are hearing about, not the agenda of the congregation itself. In a similar way, if the church expects its primary leadership to come from the board rather than from the lead pastor, what it likely does not understand is that leadership is not a group activity. What they are unwittingly buying into is primary leadership from the most influential individual on the board. The downside is that when the real leader is wearing camouflage, he or she is not identified, qualified, and held accountable for the power being wielded.

Winning churches utilize their boards to hold their primary leader accountable but not to provide that leadership itself. Chapter 8 will give more attention to the separate and complementary roles of board and lead pastor, among others. At this point we will move to a couple of examples of churches that enthusiastically answer, "The pastor!" to the big question, Who takes the lead?

Homegrown leadership credibility

For a number of years Riverside Church in Big Lake, Minnesota, was known in the Christian and Missionary Alliance as a medium-sized congregation that oscillated up and down between two hundred and four hundred in attendance. Today it is in Lyle Schaller's "very large church" category, averaging more than twelve hundred in worship and growing rapidly toward the "megachurch" level. What changed? The leadership culture of the church. It went from the typical checks-and-balances climate of suspicion to a high level of trust and support of the leadership of its senior pastor, Tom Lundeen. This transformation did not happen by itself, of course. It was prepared by the sacrificial pain of a former pastor, initiated by intentional trust-building steps by Tom in his first year, confirmed in the crucible of moral failures on staff, and maximized by implementing Accountable Leadership as an organizational strategy.

The lead pastor who preceded Tom Lundeen at Riverside had led the church through some difficult and needful changes in its worship and outreach. In the process, unfortunately, he had inadvertently burned some bridges with influential members. Like many missional leaders, he was forced out, which is a painful experience that costs congregations and denominations some of their better leaders on a regular basis. The former pastor had set the church up for growth, but it could easily have slipped back into old patterns, as it had in previous cycles.

Soon after Tom Lundeen accepted the pastorate at Riverside, he attended his first trustees meeting and brought them a minor proposal for improvement. "Oh, I'm sorry, Pastor," the chairman explained, "I guess no one told you. You are an *ex-officio* member of this board. You're here as a guest." From that point forward, Tom worked graciously but firmly to see that the dysfunctional bylaws of the church were replaced and that the leadership-wary culture of the church was confronted. His excellent communication gifts helped him amass the chips of credibility he needed to accomplish these changes. The church began to grow.

Several years into their new experience as a large, thriving church, the people at Riverside were devastated to learn of moral failures by two of the key members on Pastor Lundeen's staff. What made the resolution even more difficult was that the behavior came to light while Tom was on sabbatical at a mission station in Africa. Would the newfound fruitfulness of the church survive the blow? As a clear sign that God had indeed transformed the culture of the congregation, the worship pastor temporarily stepped up effectively to the challenge as Pastor Lundeen's representative until Tom could return. The shaken membership rallied behind their pastor and his remaining staff team as they guided the ship through the unhappy waters of discipline. And the church continued to grow and make new disciples from the community.

As part of the new approach to pastoral leadership at Riverside, the board and key staff members read and worked through the strategy of Accountable Leadership presented in my book *Winning on Purpose*. As a consultant, I had the privilege of training the board and coaching it through the creation of its Guiding Principles document. The missional alignment of the lead pastor, the executive pastor, and the board chairman at Riverside Church impressed me. If the congregation continues to value and support the strong leadership of its pastor and his team, as it has learned to do in recent years, it will make a major Kingdom impact on its community for years to come.

Thriving in a leadership-friendly tribe

By default and shortsightedness, many denominational judicatories—districts, regions, associations, conventions, and the like—do not nurture a leadership-friendly culture (more on that topic in Chapter 8), but there are a few happy exceptions. One of the best is GHC (Growing Healthy Churches), a network of congregations primarily in northern California and northwest Nevada, formerly known as the American Baptist Churches of the West. I had one of the best experiences of my career serving for a number of years as an area consultant and as director of church planting for GHC. The Accountable Leadership strategy was developed out of my previous experience as a senior pastor and out of my professional consultations with GHC churches.

One of the brightest bulbs in that bright chandelier was a lead pastor at First Baptist Church of Clovis, California, near Fresno, named Tim Brown. With the training and support of GHC, which had affected a potent pro-leadership climate among its churches, Dr. Brown led a dramatic turnaround in a congregation plagued by stagnation and church splits to healthy growth by conversions of new Christians.

In order to enhance and continue the progress of FBCC, Tim brought me in to help them implement Accountable Leadership. In this case they were ready to replace their bylaws completely with a new set designed specifically to require and support this strategy. Once the congregation approved the new structure, the pastor began a fresh learning curve to make the best use of the freedom that he and the staff now enjoyed. It was almost like a teenager being given the keys to the family car for the first time; but it was even more like a wise thirty-five-year-old driver whose overprotective mother had finally started treating him like an adult.

Tim and his leaders were looking forward to initiating greater outreach to the community and the world beyond it as well as changing the name of the church to reflect its fresh style and sense of purpose. Here is what happened.

Days after Hurricane Katrina decimated New Orleans, and not long after FBCC had adopted Accountable Leadership, the mayor of Fresno, California, who at the time happened to be a former television actor and also a committed Christian, announced that Fresno would become a city of refuge for victims of the disaster. Unfortunately, he couldn't get the political powers around him to back the idea. Not giving up so easily, he turned to a local ministerial organization to see if the churches in the region would help him make good on his promise by sponsoring evacuee families.

Call after call to local churches brought disappointing results. Each congregation had too much red tape to respond in a big way on short notice. Then Pastor Brown received his call. "Sure," he said after reflecting for a moment, "we'll do it." There was no need for process at the board or congregational level because the congregation and the board had already acted to authorize its pastor and his staff to make important decisions within predetermined parameters.

A family from New Orleans that FBCC "adopted" was set up in a free apartment and regained its hope for the future. The story was written up in the local paper, which accelerated the generosity of both the members within the congregation and of the new fans of this outreaching church that were generated by the good press in the community.

As a result of the pastor's freedom to lead decisively, several things happened. Hurting people were blessed. The congregation saw the value of its new structure. The pastor and staff gained confidence. The community saw a local church ministry at its best. Attendance growth exploded. People came to Christ. The mayor was happy.

There was only one problem. First Baptist Church discovered that it was now impossible to change its name. The public reputation attached to it had become far too valuable.

A final word on primary leaders

Leadership is not godliness; it is simply the ability to influence people toward a purpose. Good leaders make mistakes—sometimes big ones. Putting a person in a leadership role with ample support does not make that person a leader. These and other caveats are good to recognize. Nevertheless, looking to the senior pastor to take the lead is one of the hallmarks of winning churches. Less fruitful churches look to the board or the congregation to be what a group can never be: the initiating leader. What they wind up with is the unaccountable and surreptitious leadership of influential individuals by default. Primary leadership is too important to an organization for such carelessness.

In 1971, Thomas Watson Jr. had a heart attack and left IBM to recover and retire. The 1970s was a good decade at IBM even without a Watson at its helm, but shortly after the auspicious debut of the IBM Personal Computer in 1981, Watson watched from the outside a series of management missteps that brought the company to the brink of disaster by the end of the decade. Instead of the vertical integration that had helped build IBM, key components of the PC were subbed out to companies like Intel and Microsoft, which led to billions of dollars in value lost to Big Blue. Also, a misguided attempt to decentralize its business model to compete with the new digital startup firms by imitating them nearly jettisoned the natural advantages that IBM had in large-scale integration. The company posted losses of $16 billion between 1991 and 1993. Hundreds of thousands of employees lost their jobs, including the CEO.

In 1993 IBM brought on its first ever CEO from outside the company, Louis Gerstner Jr. The TV series *Biography* relates the story that on Gerstner's first day of work, a company limo pulled up to his home to collect him. When he entered the backseat, there sitting next to him was Thomas Watson Jr. It was like a scene from some Mafia movie. "Mind if I ride in to work with you?" asked Watson. It was an offer—of heartfelt and expert advice—that Gerstner couldn't refuse. Thomas Watson Jr. died later that year, a leader and maker of leaders to the end. And, by the way, Louis Gerstner succeeded in turning IBM around to health and growth.

SUMMARY AND PREVIEW

- *By looking to its lead pastor, a winning church answers the question of who takes the lead.*

- *Lack of trust as the culture of a congregation is the biggest obstacle to strong pastoral leadership. Others include false humility, denial, people pleasing, and moral failure.*

- *The nearest competing alternative to the value of a senior pastor as the leader is ostensibly the board as the leader, which in reality boils down to an influential individual on the board.*

- *A congregational culture that values pastoral leadership can be grown from within over time.*

- *The same thing can be developed more quickly with the support of a pro-leadership coaching and consultation.*

- *Strong pastoral leadership alone does not make a winning church, but no winning church is made without it.*

The next chapter shows how winning churches answer the fourth big value question: what's it going to cost?

CHAPTER FIVE

What's It Going to Cost?

No one would remember the Good Samaritan
if he'd only had good intentions; he had money as well.
Margaret Thatcher

OPERATION OVERLORD ON JUNE 6, 1944, the Allied invasion of Normandy, was the beginning of the end for Nazi Germany. More than 6,900 vessels composed the invasion fleet, including 4,100 landing craft. Some 12,000 aircraft supported the landing, including 1,000 parachute transports. A total of 10,000 tons of bombs were dropped. Roughly 150,000 troops were landed on D-Day, about half from the United States and half from the British Commonwealth countries. By July 4 more than 150,000 vehicles, 600,000 tons of supplies, and one million troops were landed. This all cost money—a lot of money.

The highest price, of course, was the cost of human lives along that fifty-mile stretch of French coastline. The Allies suffered approximately ten thousand casualties on the first day. Many plans went awry. The Americans were landed on the wrong beach and made up two-thirds of the Allied casualties. Airborne units had been dropped in wrong locations as well. The whole thing was a mess. But it worked.

High-impact ministry is often messy and costly as well. On the day of Pentecost, the apostles fanned out across the city of Jerusalem miraculously speaking the good news in languages they had never studied to people from countries they had never seen. Three thousand new disciples were added that day to the band of 120 who had gathered in the upper room to wait for the Holy Spirit. With daily growth, they soon numbered five thousand. It was instant multicultural megachurch; but expensive needs were popping up everywhere. So generous property owners among them began liquidating assets and entrusting them to the apostles and their assistants to use wisely. Life was breaking out all over, but life was—and is—messy. The alternative is neater and cheaper, but not as desirable: "Without oxen a stable stays clean, / but you need a strong ox for a large harvest" (Prov. 14:4 NLT).

I know of a church plant in the mid-1990s that grew so rapidly in its early months that the multiplication of small groups was sloppy and poorly supervised. Leaders were hastily appointed or took charge on their own. Unknown to the pastoral staff, during the chaos even a few enterprising Mormons began to host and teach small groups of the newcomers who didn't know enough yet to tell the difference. It didn't take too long to catch on and to improve the quality control, but in the meantime, what a mess! Some defenders of sound doctrine and decorum would take this incident as evidence that congregations should not be so aggressive in their outreach (which is why I'm not sharing names here). They should focus on glorifying God instead of running such risks. That's one way to look at it. When I read the Corinthian letters and reflect on the messy new congregations started by the Apostle Paul, however, I think that new babies are worth having to change poopy diapers now and then. As for serious discipleship and glorifying God, Jesus linked both of them with bearing much fruit in John 15:8.[1] And as for the church plant I described, it has made thousands of new disciples and planted a dozen or more new congregations since it cleaned up its small group roster years ago.

Good decisions use resources productively

Thus far, our look at big value questions that winning churches answer well has covered mission, authority, and leadership. When a congregation values a pastor's leadership to accomplish the mission that its Lord has prescribed, it has begun to move from theology to practice; but that is precisely the point at which tensions start to run high. Money is going to be spent. Time is going to be scheduled. People are going to be deployed. Just what is all this going to cost?

To put it simply: whatever it takes. That is the way that successful congregations look at raising and spending their resources. It is a matter of cost-effectiveness far more than price, though both of these things must be weighed and counted. This priority starts with a clear understanding of what cost-effectiveness really means.

On one hand, the term *cost-benefit*, as used in the business world, is monetary on both ends. In other words, this analysis compares the amount of money that goes in up front to the amount of money that comes out in the end. It is all about return on investment, whether measured in dollars, euros, or yen. As such, it is not an appropriate basis for evaluating ministry. Why not? Because, unlike a business, the church does not exist to make a financial profit for its owners. We have already established that it exists to accomplish the will of its Lord, and he doesn't need money. He desires something more precious: human beings brought into his family.

The specific concept of *cost-effectiveness*, on the other hand, is highly appropriate for use in the church. This kind of analysis compares one plan to use resources against another designed to accomplish the same end. That end need not be financial. For example, let's say a congregation wants to see a thriving student ministry developed to engage at least 75 percent of the high schoolers whose parents attend worship. One plan is to spend 25 percent of existing staff hours on an ongoing basis to recruit and train many volunteer workers. A second plan is to raise or borrow a year's salary to hire a dynamic youth pastor with a track record of success. Plan three is to budget heavily for conferences, clerical support, and expense accounts to attract and equip three volunteer staff people. Each of these options will cost money, offset to some degree by growth. Which of them will accomplish the most for the same amount of money?

It's bang for the buck that winning churches want, not bucks for the buck. Let's look at some real-world examples, from great congregations, of smart money for God.

Raise the rent

Bishop Silas Ng, introduced earlier in the book, founded an evangelistic Anglican congregation in Richmond, British Columbia, to reach Chinese Canadians. Though the launch of Richmond Emmanuel Church was successful, every year brought difficulties to overcome. One of these was the challenge of adequate space. The first meeting place of the new ministry was an Anglican church building belonging to a Caucasian congregation; on Sunday this was only available in the afternoon. A few years later Richmond Emmanuel rented a warehouse owned by a private institute for mathematics. Both of these facilities were very low rent and met the needs of the group for a limited period of time.

After two years in the warehouse facility, Bishop Ng led his large congregation to take a bold step forward to a location that can accommodate them with room to grow. The former Richmond City Hall building provides twenty-four thousand square feet and came with a price tag that initially brought a fair bit of sticker shock to bear. It was a risk at that time. Bishop Ng had seen God provide at earlier points of need, however, and was confident he would do so again. He was right.

Bring on the planters

The vision of Pastor Louis Bourque's church north of Montreal was also introduced in Chapter 2. The church is planting ten new Francophone congregations in Quebec over ten years. Carrying out this plan takes a lot of money, which is primarily invested in church-planting interns and coaches.

Because far less than 1 percent of the population across the province has an affiliation with any evangelical church, Quebec has been called the least-reached people-group in North America.[2] As this level of need is made known abroad, the dollars and hours invested by Louis's people are able to attract a large infusion of mission giving from Christians in the rest of Canada and in the United States. The combination has been able to produce more new church-planting pastors and more new congregations than would otherwise be possible.

Extreme makeover

Some two thousand miles to the south, in Tallahassee, Florida, Pastor Mark McNees a few years ago faced a dilemma common to successful new church plants: where to put all the people. Already meeting in three packed services in a leased retail space, the edgy, outreaching church known as "Element 3" was growing well in both human and financial terms. Its mission focus was on connecting with the emerging generations that had not found a place in traditional or boomer congregations across the city.[3] Some of the other churches in town had originally begun with an outward focus to make new disciples but had turned inward over the years. Other local churches stayed true to the Great Commission but appealed more to other demographics than to the new crop of postmoderns coming on the scene.

Early as it was in E3's development, it could have relocated to a larger leased space that was less well located. Mark and his team could even have pondered buying and building at the expense of diverting attention from the formative stages of their ministry. Instead they chose to mount a capital campaign to expand and renovate their current leased facility, which had been a restaurant with adjacent retail bays.

True, E3 will one day leave most of those expensive improvements behind. I'm sure the project raised an eyebrow or two at the beginning. The ability to get room to grow quickly, however, without rolling the dice on a new location or assuming the burden of major construction made the decision highly cost-effective for both short-term and long-term purposes. E3 may not wait to build until they hit ten thousand attendees as Saddleback did, but it is following the same priority of people first and property later.

In tent on a mission

Moving from one citrus-growing state to another, First Baptist Church of Clovis, California, had experienced a major turnaround under the leadership of Dr. Tim Brown. His effectiveness and the model that supports it were described in Chapter 4. With a newfound outward focus, the church grew to seven hundred in multiple services and decided to hold its Easter service each year as one big outreach event at a convention center.

One particular year, the facility management threw FBCC a nasty curve by canceling their signed contract shortly before the big day. The decision structure allowed Tim to act quickly, and he opted to have a large rented tent erected on the church property for Easter. This was no wedding reception pavilion; it was more like a circus tent without the clowns. At $10,000, it was not a judgment call for the faint of heart. The tent provided one thousand seats, but twelve thousand people showed up.

As it turned out, someone who had not supported the church in the past paid the entire cost with a single gift that day.

Cheap, cheap, cheap is for the birds

Winning churches answer the question, What's it going to cost? with "Whatever it takes." That is not the way all congregations think. In fact, it is not the way most congregations think, unfortunately. So what is the nearest competing value to this winning value?

Wasting money by spending large amounts without the intended results is, of course, an alternative to cost-effectiveness. That folly, however, is normally so obvious that it is not a real threat except in zero-accountability scenarios flush with cash. For the vast majority of churches the value that rises to the top by default regarding money is the instinct to hold on to as much of it as possible. This shows up in two primary ways in church decisions.

One way is simply paying as little as possible without considering the upside and downside consequences of every option. "Penny wise and pound foolish" is the English idiom that marks this instinct. It leads shortsighted churches to use pulpit supply instead of an interim pastor, to grant two-week rather than four-week vacations, and to erect metal-sided buildings in upscale communities. Saving money is great, but the apparent price might be deceptively lower than the real cost. A small church in decline kept its air conditioner off one summer to save money. "You'll get used to it," said a friendly member to my sister-in-law, who was visiting with her baby. She didn't return—and neither did her pocketbook.

The other manifestation of "How low can we go?" in churches is putting the highest priority on being debt free. No question—debt involves obligation, and too much of it is burdensome to the point of bondage. In some circumstances, however, the limited use of borrowed capital is the best way to get something accomplished at the time that it is needed. My father built our family home with his own hands and never had a mortgage. It gave him the opportunity to make other investments, and I will always admire his determination. Years later, when his grandson, my nephew, planned to follow his example, however, my dad advised against it. "You spend all those years building it for your family," he said, "and by the time you're done, they're moving out."

There is no book that can tell your church the right amount to spend, how much of it to borrow, and what it should buy. There are too many variables in the real world of ministry for that. What can be made clear, however, is that highly fruitful congregations choose to pay whatever it takes to accomplish the mission. That is more important to them than paying as little as possible.

Maybe rowboats and slingshots would have been cheaper than the arsenal unleashed on D-Day; but it would have cost too much to save the money.

SUMMARY AND PREVIEW

- *Congregations that win long term aim to make decisions that use resources cost-effectively.*

- *Taking a calculated risk to pay more can pay off.*

- *Giving that encourages others to give makes more ministry possible.*

- *A strategic expense in the near term can protect the long term.*

- *Spending for events that reach people can pay for themselves.*

- *The competing value to cost-effectiveness is low price at any cost.*

The next chapter addresses the big question, What if there's trouble? If this never happens at your church, you may skip it.

CHAPTER SIX

What If There's Trouble?

THE ELOI WERE HAVING SUCH A NICE PICNIC by the river on that day in the year 802,701 when George arrived from nineteenth-century England in his time machine. He had traveled hundreds of millennia to find out what would become of the human race. The specimens before him, the Eloi, quickly impressed George with their carefree, gentle nature as they laughed and played. They were all flaxen-haired young adults in soft pastel tunics. The future was looking very pleasant—or at least very blonde.

Suddenly a young woman fell into the rapid current of the river, and she could not swim. She cried out and clutched desperately at a large rock where a few of her companions were sitting. They glanced down at her with a nod and a smile and continued their banter without lifting a finger to save her. George raced down to the river's edge, shed his Victorian jacket, and dove in to rescue the girl. After he had dragged her safely to the shore, he gaped in astonishment as she too resumed the blissful expression and passive behavior of her companions, strolling slowly off into the woods without a word of thanks.

That scene, from a 1960 film adaptation of *The Time Machine* by H. G. Wells, reminds me of the passive-aggressive behavior through which church folk sometimes sell God's purposes and one another down the river. It's called denial.

The last big value question that winning churches answer differently from churches on the rocks follows logically after, What must be done? Who says so? Who takes the lead? and What's it going to cost? Even if we get all those right—what if there's trouble?

Good decisions confront dysfunction

The prophet Nehemiah is well known for mobilizing God's people to accomplish a mission in spite of recurring opposition, both overt and covert. His mission was to lead the people of Jerusalem, who had returned from their exile in Babylon in recent years, to rebuild the wall of the city. It was a matter of life and death. The wall of an ancient city was the only thing that separated its inhabitants from the worst things that their hostile neighbors could do to them, and Jerusalem's wall was still a heap of scorched rubble from its destruction some seventy years earlier. Nehemiah's resistance to the schemes of his opponents has a familiar ring to many a pastor:

> When word came to Sanballat, Tobiah, Geshem the Arab, and the rest of our enemies that I had rebuilt the wall and not a gap was left in it—though up to that time I had not set the doors in the gates—Sanballat and Geshem sent me this message: "Come, let us meet together in one of the villages on the plain of Ono."
>
> But they were scheming to harm me; so I sent messengers to them with this reply: "I am carrying on a great project and cannot go down. Why should the work stop while I leave it and go down to you?" Four times they sent me the same message, and each time I gave them the same answer.
>
> Then, the fifth time, Sanballat sent his aide to me with the same message, and in his hand was an unsealed letter in which was written:
>
> "It is reported among the nations—and Geshem says it is true—that you and the Jews are plotting to revolt, and therefore you are building the wall. Moreover, according to these reports you are about to become

their king and have even appointed prophets to make this proclamation about you in Jerusalem: 'There is a king in Judah!' Now this report will get back to the king; so come, let us meet together."

I sent him this reply: "Nothing like what you are saying is happening; you are just making it up out of your head."

They were all trying to frighten us, thinking, "Their hands will get too weak for the work, and it will not be completed."

But I prayed, "Now strengthen my hands." (Neh. 6:1-9)

How many vehicles for deception and manipulation can you count in the story? There is the invitation to a meeting, which is obviously a setup. There is repetition, the same demand four or five times, designed to wear the leader down. There is the open letter to fan the flames of public sentiment. There is the exaggerated scope of criticism—"It is reported among the nations"—and the manufactured authority—"and Geshem says it is true." There is the big lie of Nehemiah rebelling against King Artaxerxes of Persia, who in fact had authorized and paid for Nehemiah's project. And finally there is the *pièce de résistance*, the feigned concern for Nehemiah's reputation if word somehow gets back to the king—not that Sanballat and friends would ever let that happen. Ono!

Nehemiah seems lucky to have these men looking out for him. They are just thinking of his protection. He better hurry on down to meet with them for his own good—not!

Winning churches follow the lead of Nehemiah's approach when political trouble rears its ugly head. They confront the dysfunction as needed to stay on mission. The prophet refused to be diverted from the purpose to which God had called him. He ignored repeated distractions. He brought false gossip out of the shadows and into the sunshine of the truth where it could be exposed for what it was. And when he and his followers were faced with intimidation, he prayed for greater strength. That's what a godly leader does.

Taking one to the chest

Element 3, led by Mark McNees in Tallahassee, was introduced in the last chapter. In fewer than ten years E3 has become a large, vibrant success story with a community presence through its midtown café, multiple worship services, and church planting projects under way. But none of this was guaranteed in its earliest days, and if its founding pastor had lacked the courage of his convictions, none of it would have happened.

Mark moved his family from southern California to north Florida out of a strong sense of call to establish a special kind of church. Although it would welcome people of every background, it would focus on the new generations of adults emerging in a city dominated by universities and government. The message would be biblical and uncompromising, but its expression would be contextualized to an increasingly postmodern culture.

The first people to join the group launching E3 had come from a recently failed church plant there in Tallahassee. They brought a few

pieces of equipment, a few good contacts, and one deep-pocketed controller. We'll call him "Biff." Mark had told the little group on his initial visit that when he returned, the old corporation would be dissolved and its lease for a space on the northwest outskirts of town would not be renewed. Biff had other ideas. He liked that location. So while the McNees family was moving across the country, Biff took it on himself to renew the lease. After all, he gave far more money than anyone else. What could this new kid from California really do about it?

The pastor arrived, found out what Biff had done, and informed him that the new church would not be using the space he had leased for it. "Oh, yes, it will be meeting there," Biff said, poking his index finger into the pastor's chest. "You need me." Pastor McNees looked the wealthy man in the eye and assured him, "We don't need you, and God doesn't need your money." Biff walked away from the church plant with his index finger, his money, and a lease that he had signed in his own name when he was sure he would have his way.

Release the hostages

George Bullard writes of a situation where a controlling personality was confronted with his help as a consultant. A planning retreat was held for the congregation to consider a proposal to relocate its facilities. Bullard realized that a particular man would likely react inappropriately in front of the entire group to such a move. When the plan was proposed, he tried to take over the meeting, standing up and raising his voice. Bullard confronted him firmly, and he walked out of the meeting along with his wife. For the next hour, Bullard debriefed the remainder of the congregation on the situation.

> Many people present acknowledged they had always refused to confront this controlling manager because he was partially right in his accusations of them. . . . However, they knew they were at a crossroads in the life of the congregation and must act on their collective courage to change the congregation's situation.

A month later the congregation voted by more than one hundred to six to relocate. They relocated within the year to a place for which they had a clear focus, purpose, and vision. Within two years they had more than tripled in size, and now fifteen years later continue a positive, passionate ministry in their new location.

Bullard relates that the antagonist and his wife, along with two other couples, left and joined another congregation. Two other couples followed them. There they became supportive members and have not tried to hold anyone hostage to their opinions. The courage to act properly brought a new opportunity of freedom for everyone involved.[1]

Bored on the board

A very large church in Texas (yes, there are some) had rapidly expanded its outreach to the community after adopting Accountable Leadership. The pastor and staff had greater freedom to move quickly on needs and opportunities. This freedom to act was starting to pay off for the church.

However, one man on the board who owned a number of restaurant franchises was accustomed to managing rather than governing. He accepted the switch to governance superficially, but he insisted on putting management issues on the board's agenda so that he could weigh in on them.

Despite the man's intimidating presence, the rest of the board found the courage to ask him to step down. He reluctantly did so and fortunately reconciled with others well enough to remain in the church family with good relationships.

Wait a minute, Mr. Postman

Leith Anderson, lead pastor at Wooddale Church, once received a series of long letters while he was away for the month of July. The groom who wrote them had reacted so badly during the course of premarital counseling when challenged about his sexual behavior that the staff pastor in charge called off the wedding. Instead of dignifying the letters, Leith wrote a simple reply: "Dear So and So: Your letters of June 23 and following have been forwarded to me while I am away, and I am writing to acknowledge the receipt of those letters. Sincerely, Leith Anderson."

On Leith's first Sunday back, the man challenged him after church. The conversation went as follows:

"You didn't read my letters!"

"Sure, I read them."

"But I wrote a lot of things in them. You didn't answer me."

"Sure, I did. I sent you a letter."

"Yeah, but it was a form letter."

"No, it wasn't. It was a personal letter."

"But it was only two lines long."

"That was all I had to say."

"Well, we need to get together to straighten this out. We need to get together tomorrow."

"I don't think so."

"Well, then, when can you get together with me?"

"I'm not going to get together with you."

The angry man proceeded to insist that the pastor had to meet with him and, when denied, began shouting and drawing a small crowd. The pastor finally did arrange a meeting—he met with his board to disfellowship the individual. The bylaws of this healthy congregation had a simple requirement for membership that supported the pastor's responsibility to confront divisive behavior: "An agreement to abide by Wooddale Church policies on Member discipline." Pastor Anderson spoke truth to dysfunction, knowing that his board members would not entertain such angry accusations.[2]

Unfaithful wounds

When faced with trouble, winning churches place the highest value on speaking the truth in love. That value is essential for a body of believers to mature in Christ, according to Ephesians 4:15. It requires upholding the integrity of board, pastor, staff, and membership. It requires thwarting gossip and other triangulation. It requires calm confrontation of manipulative behavior. Large thriving churches are not immune from dysfunction, but they are quick to identify and correct it. "Wounds from a friend can be trusted, / but an enemy multiplies kisses" (Prov. 27:6).

What is the nearest competing value to speaking the truth in love? It is speaking inoffensively. This is a good thing when possible, but not as important as truth and love. One soft-spoken denominational executive, for example, was brought in to mediate a conflict between an associate pastor and a church board after a prolonged vacuum of power (no lead pastor or interim on staff). After many meetings where much was said but little was resolved, a public reconciliation service was held—complete with foot washing. At a follow-up meeting with the congregation, the mediator reassured them by saying rosily, "I have not met one angry person in this church." Such sweet words. The consultant drove away, and the unconfronted dysfunction continued to increase the conflict level in the church.

Dysfunctional behavior does not go away by denying it or appeasing it. Nehemiah had to fend off challenges to the vision repeatedly, sometimes from the same individuals. Pastors and boards need to follow his example. As British Prime Minister Margaret Thatcher, the Iron Lady, once said, "You may have to fight a battle more than once to win it."

SUMMARY AND PREVIEW

- *When there's trouble, winning congregations correct dysfunction.*

- *Nehemiah's story is a classic example of overcoming dysfunctional behavior.*

- *God doesn't need the money of manipulative donors.*

- *The right consultant can help a church confront dysfunction.*

- *A courageous board can confront an overcontrolling member.*

- *Wise lead pastors with a healthy board's support can address dysfunction without having to watch their own backs.*

In Part 2 we move from values to practices. It begins with a chapter on the fine art of application.

PART TWO

THEN GET THE DEVIL OUT OF THE DETAILS

CHAPTER SEVEN

The Art of Application

As I grow older,
I pay less attention to what men say.
I just watch what they do.
Andrew Carnegie

SOUTHWEST AIRLINES HAD A SERIOUS PROBLEM. At 10:00 in the morning, just two days before the low-cost carrier was supposed to initiate service to San Diego, Southwest finally received a building permit from the Port Authority to renovate their main ticket counter. Red tape had delayed the approval process. The flight schedule had long been published. Time had run out. There was no way to do the construction work and be open for business in two days. Five minutes after receiving the overdue permit, however, airline employees removed a temporary screen of drywall to reveal a completed ticket counter that had already been built behind it. The personnel on scene gambled on the permit coming through and ran the risk of having to dismantle the unsanctioned construction if need be. The work could not be done in two days, but it *could* simply appear in five minutes because Southwest Airlines places value on flexible action rather than on consistent protocol. Because of this, its people were able to solve the urgent problem.

For Southwest, the creativity that got its San Diego service up and running is not restricted to this isolated event. Big decisions settled early on for the company resulted in a clear and compelling set of values that its better employees simply apply to whatever situations they happen to face. New personnel who are unaccustomed to its agile corporate culture, even seasoned executives, soon find themselves in a whole new world. On one occasion, the new marketing vice president, Don Valentine, who had come from Dr Pepper, outlined his suggested timetable for a new TV advertising campaign: draft the script by March and approve it in April; cast the commercial in June and begin production in September. "Don, I hate to tell you," responded Southwest cofounder Herb Kelleher, at the campaign team meeting, "but we're talking about next Wednesday."[1]

It's one thing to have a clearly defined set of values. It's another to let them guide behavior in one decision after another. Whether at the airport or at the parish, what we are talking about is the fine art of application.

Review of the big five

Part 1 explored five major questions that every church faces and that successful churches answer differently from others. Before moving forward into examples of their application, let's review the big questions along with their answers. Table 7.1 below contains each of the big five, followed by the essential answer chosen by highly fruitful congregations in comparison with the most relevant competing answer:

TABLE 7.1—REVIEW OF THE BIG FIVE

Value Question	Winning Answer	Competing Answer
#1: What must be done?	Make new disciples	Serve the members
#2: Who says so?	Christ, the Owner	Influential stakeholders
#3: Who takes the lead?	The lead pastor	Influential board members
#4: What's it going to cost?	Whatever it takes	As little as possible
#5: What if there's trouble?	Speak truth in love	Speak inoffensively

The first and most obvious choice concerns the purpose of our existence as a local expression of the body of Christ. Winning churches are committed to a missional response, an outwardly focused response. Think first of those who do not yet know Christ. Make disciples. The path of least resistance that most congregations take is to make member care the higher priority, if not in word then at least in behavior.

When the purpose of the ministry is challenged, the second big question goes to the source of authority. Mission is not the most comfortable answer to question number one. The most comfortable answer—to serve the members of the church—emanates from the most influential stakeholders in the church, whether or not they are in official leadership. In order to stand firm for mission, it is essential to honor the ultimate ownership of the congregation by its Lord and Head, Jesus Christ. He directed his followers to make disciples of all ethnicities. He alone has the right to determine the purpose of his church.

Once the questions of what must be done and how we know what must be done are settled, the next instinct is to look around the room, so to speak, and ask: Who takes the lead? To whom do we look for initiative and guidance? Larger, growing churches inevitably depend on a highly effective lead pastor to take the point. Decisions will be made in such a way as to reinforce trust in the designated shepherd of the flock. The most likely competing answer, one that characterizes most stable and shrinking congregations with a significant number of constituents, is one or more influential board members. The board itself may be thought of as the competing answer, but the idea of the board as a whole providing the initiating leadership is an illusion. Groups do not lead; they are led. If the pastor is not setting the pace on the board, one or another individual on the board is playing that role.

With the imperative being mission, the authority being Christ, and the leader being the pastor, question number four concerns the means to implement the mission under the pastor's leadership: what's it going to cost? Mediocre congregations focus on price. Excellent congregations focus on cost-effectiveness. No one wants to waste resources, but better to spend a little too much on what works than to save a little too much on what doesn't.

Finally, question number five takes us from the positive side of implementation to the unpleasant side: overcoming opposition. What if there's trouble? What will we do in the face of conflict? The easy choice is to keep the peace and to speak as inoffensively as possible. Don't risk ruffling feathers, driving away people, or—bottom line—losing income. Thriving congregations know that it's healthier to make peace that is authentic than it is to keep the peace that is unworthy of its name. They choose to speak the truth in love. Dysfunction is graciously but firmly uprooted whenever it rears its ugly head.

Values without application aren't values

Several years ago I spoke at a one-day training event based on my first book, *Winning on Purpose*. The event was for about four hundred pastors in a denominational gathering. The morning session was a straight presentation of the organizational strategy I call "Accountable Leadership." The early afternoon session was a lively discussion, which I merely observed, led by a panel of larger-church pastors focused on how they were adapting and implementing what they called "the Kaiser model"—pretty heady stuff for a new author. The late afternoon was devoted to questions and answers. I'll never forget one of the questions presented to me in writing that day: How can we help people in our congregation live by their real values? "That's easy," I replied. "People always live by their real values."

The choices covered in Part 1 are by far the most important decisions discussed in this book. If, however, the answers to those fundamental questions are not translated into the kinds of strategic and tactical decisions touched upon in Part 2, they were never the real answers of a church to begin with. So it is time to take up the practical implications of the big five for the teeming host of smaller choices that comprise ministry in the field.

Overview of Part 2

Chapter 8 deals with the roles played by various key individuals or groups in the highly fruitful congregation. People are not always going to agree with a given decision, so it is necessary to establish just who will decide what. If we have agreement on the question, Whose call is that one? it will be easier to live with and support choices that we might not have made had we worn the shoes of the decider. When should the congregation weigh in on a decision? What is important for the board to handle? What is best left to the lead pastor to determine? Which decisions should be pushed to the staff members as they serve on the front line week to week? How does the denomination or movement to which our congregation relates—or *tribe* for shorthand—influence the choices that are legitimate within the commitments that tie the two together? Each of these roles will be treated in turn.

TABLE 7.2—LESSONS ON GETTING THE DEVIL OUT OF THE DETAILS

Chapter	Winning churches . . .
8: Who Decides What	have cleaner decision-making roles
9: Best Practices for Typical Decisions	use better ways and means
10: A Catalog of Dysfunctions to Avoid	avoid self-defeating games

After examining each of the decision-making roles, we turn in **Chapter 9** to look at fifteen of the most common types of significant decisions that local churches make in the course of doing ministry. Some of these, like budgets and programming, come around with regularity. Others, like building programs and bylaws, come up less often. Some, like dismissing a lead pastor, are hopefully rare if not purely theoretical. Others, like power struggles and church discipline, are unpleasant but to be expected. A few, like hiring a lead pastor or starting a new congregation, are exciting and expanding. Each of the fifteen types of decisions included tend to be handled somewhat or very differently by thriving congregations than by stagnant ones.

Turning the tables from best practices, **Chapter 10** comprises a catalog of decision-making dysfunctions to avoid. Such a compilation could be as long as the possibilities of human folly are numerous. The approach taken in a limited space is to offer a top ten list of "don'ts" related to each of the five decision-making roles: lead pastor, staff, board, congregation, and tribe. Even at fifty individual items, the catalog is suggestive rather than exhaustive.

"The devil is in the details," goes the old saying. As Table 7.2 depicts, the learning points in Part 2 are arranged to help roust him out of there. Thriving churches think and act differently from the pack. They distinguish decision-making roles more cleanly, use better ways and means, and avoid dysfunction like the plague. Congregations who would join their ranks must learn to do the same.

Every context is the same: it's unique

Having searched YouTube in vain for my favorite pickle commercial of all time, in this case probably from the early 1970s, here is the dialogue to the best of my memory:

> Little boy, hiding a dog behind him: "Dad, can I have a dog?"
> Father, hiding his face behind a newspaper: "No!"
> Boy: "Didn't you have a dog when you were my age?"
> Father: "Things were different then."
> Boy: "Aren't things different now?"
> Father: "No, they're the same!"
> Boy: "Then can I have a dog?"

At which point the boy strategically plops a pickle in his father's mouth to soften him up and show him the dog, already in tow. Every context of ministry for decision making is the same in one important way as well: it is different. Each congregation functions with a unique mix of time, place, culture, strengths, weaknesses, opportunities, and threats.

This uniqueness is helpful to keep in mind when reading the chapters that follow. The best application of cost-effectiveness, for example, will vary greatly from one socioeconomic context to another. One group's necessity will be another group's luxury—all a matter of perception. No doubt even in similar contexts there is more than one good way to live out the right values in many decision scenarios. Hopefully, however, there are enough ideas in Part 2 to illustrate the kinds of tactics to be preferred.

SUMMARY AND PREVIEW

- *It is one thing to choose a value and another thing to apply it.*

- *A review of the big five values highlights mission over member care, Christ over stakeholders, lead pastor over influential board members, cost-effectiveness over low cost, and peacemaking over peacekeeping.*

- *Values not applied through behavior are not one's real values.*

- *Part 2 covers decision roles, decision types, and decision dysfunctions.*

- *Every ministry context is unique, but enough ideas should yield some help for any context.*

The next chapter examines the respective roles of congregation, lead pastor, board, staff, and tribe (denomination or movement) in the decision-making process.

CHAPTER EIGHT

Who Decides What

No institution can possibly survive
if it needs geniuses or supermen to manage it.
It must be organized in such a way as to be able to get along
under a leadership composed of average human beings.
Peter Drucker

GETTING ADVICE FROM YOUR FATHER-IN-LAW must rank up there with getting a colonoscopy. It can be embarrassing to the point of humiliation, but if it's done right, you just might learn something that you really needed to know. That's the way it was for Moses back in the day. Though he had originally protested his inability to speak in public, things had changed. After launching ten plagues, parting the Red Sea, and getting water from rocks in the desert, Moses must have come to believe he knew what he was doing as a leader. And he probably did not think it all came from having a great staff. So when his wife's father, Jethro, came to visit, Moses may have been eager to show him how hard he was working and how important he was to all the people. The book of Exodus tells the story:

> Jethro was delighted to hear about all the good things the LORD had done for Israel in rescuing them from the hand of the Egyptians. . . .
> The next day Moses took his seat to serve as judge for the people, and they stood around him from morning till evening. When his father-in-law saw all that Moses was doing for the people, he said, "What is this you are doing for the people? Why do you alone sit as judge, while all these people stand around you from morning till evening?"
> Moses answered him, "Because the people come to me to seek God's will. Whenever they have a dispute, it is brought to me, and I decide between the parties and inform them of God's decrees and instructions."

Moses' father-in-law replied, "What you are doing is not good. You and these people who come to you will only wear yourselves out. The work is too heavy for you; you cannot handle it alone. Listen now to me and I will give you some advice, and may God be with you. You must be the people's representative before God and bring their disputes to him. Teach them his decrees and instructions, and show them the way they are to live and how they are to behave. But select capable men from all the people—men who fear God, trustworthy men who hate dishonest gain—and appoint them as officials over thousands, hundreds, fifties and tens. Have them serve as judges for the people at all times, but have them bring every difficult case to you; the simple cases they can decide themselves. That will make your load lighter, because they will share it with you. If you do this and God so commands, you will be able to stand the strain, and all these people will go home satisfied." (Exod. 18:9, 13-23)

Not only did his father-in-law give excellent advice, Moses actually followed it. Those must be two of the greatest miracles in the Pentateuch—*manna live!* Like Moses, the lead pastors of winning churches know that a smart division of labor is needed to accomplish a great purpose with God's people. In this chapter we will look at the best roles that the congregation, the lead pastor, the board, the staff, and the tribe can play. By *tribe*, we borrow Lyle Schaller's shorthand for *denomination* and extend it to include whatever movement, formal or informal, with which a congregation identifies itself.

The tribe decides what to reinforce

Before a board or a lead pastor exercises any decision-making authority, they must be granted that authority legitimately. Who does the granting? The question may be viewed from both a legal and an ecclesiastical perspective. From a legal point of view, legitimate authority flows to the officers of the corporation from the membership of the corporation. For that reason, from an ecclesiastical point of view, a church must make it a point to identify and position its legal membership with care in relation to its officers.

Although the Christian community is composed of various tribes (i.e., denominations, affiliations, or movements), there is no controversy over who is the Head of the church: Jesus Christ. There are, however, considerable differences among the tribes as to how Christ is believed to impart his authority to the leaders of his church. Each tribe has its own polity. Historically speaking, the three major polities are *episcopal* (a hierarchy of overseers or bishops), *presbyterian* (a hierarchy of councils or courts), and *congregational* (no hierarchy above the local membership). Table 8.1 outlines the way each polity would view the transmission of Christ's authority to the leaders of a local congregation.[1]

There are variations and hybrids of these structures in some tribes, but we will emphasize the three major polity options here. A congregational church will most likely equate the members of the corporation with the members of the church of voting age. In that way, the ecclesiastical structure of the church will align with the legal structure of its corporation. A church with presbyterian polity may equate the members of the local corporation with the members of its board or *session*, the council of lead pastor and other elders who rule a congregation. Or it could equate church members as corporation members with limited rights. Either way, its legal charter[2] would subordinate the local corporation to that of the *presbytery* or *classis* in the area, the next highest council of pastors and elders. A congregation in an episcopal denomination may or may not equate church members and corporation members, but again its charter would define the congregation as a local branch of a larger church under the supervision of a territorial overseer such as a *bishop* or *district superintendent*.

Having traced some key differences in church polity, a certain reality check is in order, one that winning churches of every tribe recognize and utilize: all churches are congregational, all churches are presbyterian, and all churches are episcopal. What? Regardless of what the documents say,

TABLE 8.1—HOW EACH POLITY VIEWS AUTHORIZATION

Polity	How Christ authorizes the local pastor and board
Congregational (members rule)	Christ speaks through the members of his body, the church. The members choose pastor and board, and delegate authority. The pastor is accountable to the members, often through the board. Each local congregation is the highest human authority under Christ.
Presbyterian (councils rule)	Christ guides councils of pastors and elders. Each council has authority over the council below it. The pastor leads the board and is accountable to the area council. The national council is the highest human authority under Christ.
Episcopal (overseers rule)	Christ gave authority to the first overseers, his apostles. Overseers transmit authority to new overseers and supervise them. The pastor leads the board and is accountable to the area overseer. The primary overseer is the highest human authority under Christ.

the people always vote. They vote with their feet and they vote with their wallets, even if they have never heard of *Robert's Rules of Order*. In that sense, all churches are congregational. Also, groups of pastors and other leaders work in council with one another at local, regional, national, and global levels whether or not they are fans of John Knox and the legacy of elder rule that he passed on from Geneva to Scotland and beyond. In that sense, all churches are presbyterian. Finally, individual primary leaders make or break every congregation, judicatory, denomination, and movement; it makes no difference if they do it with rings to kiss or bare knuckles. "Everything rises and falls on leadership," says John Maxwell.[3] In that sense, every church is episcopal.

With the differences and commonalities above in mind, what is the essential contribution to good decision making that any tribe can bring to one of its congregations? From the local perspective, how does the tribe factor into the critical choices a winning church makes? The truth is, in the real world it rarely does at all. Sadly, in most cases the larger, growing congregation is an exception to the rule in its denomination and does not find much real help available there. Denominational executives are frequently drawn from the loyal rank and file. Growth-oriented pastors of large churches either decline to accept such roles or they do not last long when they do accept them and attempt to bring change. There are two kinds of tribal affiliations that can assist the local church, however. One is the resource-based network, which congregations can easily join and depart based on the help being provided. These have become ubiquitous, especially in connection with the proliferation of megachurches in the United States. These networks, such as the Willow Creek Association or Acts 29 Network, can either replace or be layered on top of a congregation's historical affiliation. The other helpful affiliation, very rare by contrast, is the turnaround judicatory. In a precious few places, courageous visionary leaders have led complete reinventions of denominational associations in decline. Growing Healthy Churches in northern California and Union Baptist Association in Houston, Texas, come to mind.[4]

When it is at its best, a tribe can make the following contributions to the decision making of a thriving congregation. At a minimum it can accredit the lead pastor and the church itself, based on the common values and standards of the tribe. This is akin to branding. It helps a bit for people to be assured that a local ministry and its leader are in good standing with a larger movement that maintains a certain integrity. More actively, tribal leaders can, if they have the nerve and expertise, come into the local church to stand up for the lead pastor in times of difficult transformational leadership. All too often, such representatives leave their best pastors out on a limb to succeed or fail. They rarely risk the reputation and mission income of the denomination by backing up the pastor when he or she needs it most. Finally, a tribe can provide resources to the pastor and board on leadership issues, which is best done by brokering state-of-the-art tools not limited to the denominational press.

The church decides on the decision makers

What kinds of choices do highly fruitful churches tend to make on a churchwide basis? How does that set of choices tend to differ from the practices of stagnant and declining churches? Having already considered the difference that polity makes for one tribe or another's particular emphasis on the congregational decision making, let's look at the best contribution the body can make to effective decisions in the church.

Whether by formal vote or otherwise, it is essential that the members of the church form a critical mass of support behind the church's leadership. As an oft-cited proverb says, "If you think you are leading and no one is following, then you are only taking a walk."[5] The things most important for a congregation to decide are (1) the decision-making process that will be used to guide its church, and (2) the individuals who will serve as lead pastor and board members.

Most congregations will at some point register an official vote in some form on the calling or confirmation of a lead pastor and board members. Congregational polity will require that they also approve the bylaws to set a leadership and decision-making structure in place. Congregations with presbyterian or episcopal polity will operate under a book of church order or discipline and will have less say about their basic structure, but they may still have some flexibility on how to apply it. In any case, all church members give or withhold their consent to the structure and leaders.

Legitimizing the decision-making process and the top decision-making leaders are the essential contributions that congregations make in successful churches. This may be accomplished by raising a hand, saying aye, or checking a box; it may simply be done by continuing to fill the seats and the offering plates. In any case, wise leaders of growing churches fully appreciate their need to mobilize a critical mass of the church family in order to achieve anything of significance.

Other broad decisions—beyond the confirmation of lead pastor and board members and the approval of bylaws—are often ratified by the membership, especially but not exclusively in congregational churches. These may include the annual budget in broad categories, acceptance of new members, and the purchase or sale of the main church property. High-impact churches rarely bring lesser decisions than these to the membership.

Table 8.2 depicts the essential contribution of the congregation to effective decision making in comparison to that of the other four roles. The more growth oriented a church is, the fewer decisions are made by the membership level beyond its essential legitimization of leadership. The cause and effect most likely works in both directions. Larger churches cannot operate effectively without entrusting most of the critical choices to its leadership. Smaller churches are hindered from becoming large churches by not thinking and acting like large churches.

The pastor decides the strategic direction

No relationship influences a church's chance of succeeding more than that of the flock to its shepherd, the lead pastor. Because larger churches place such a high value on their primary leader, as discussed in Chapter 4, they are careful to set up the engagement of their pastor with other decision makers in an intentional manner. To better understand the central role of the lead pastor both in making decisions and in leading others who make decisions, consider the relative level of decision types on a spectrum from strategic to tactical, to use a military analogy. Most would recognize

TABLE 8.2—DECISION-MAKING ROLES IN WINNING CHURCHES

Role	Essential Contributions	Level	Verb
Congregation	Consents to decision-making process Consents to lead pastor and board	Support	Legitimize
Lead Pastor	Leads board to decide grand strategy Makes strategic decisions Leads staff to decide operations Leads congregation to support vision Represents congregation to tribe	Strategy	Lead
Board	Makes mission and boundary decisions Monitors performance of lead pastor	Grand Strategy	Govern
Staff	Makes operational decisions as a team Makes and delegates tactical decisions	Operations and Tactics	Manage
Tribe	Endorses the lead pastor and church Provides resources to the lead pastor and board	Reinforcement	Consult

that strategic plans have broader implications than tactical plans. There are actually four distinct levels, however, comprised in the full spectrum of military decision making: grand strategy, strategy, operations, and tactics.

Grand strategy refers to the ultimate geopolitical goals of a nation as they relate to defense or warfare. During World War II, for example, part of the Allies' grand strategy was to achieve the total (i.e., not negotiated) surrender of Germany and Japan within the limits of a policy of Europe first, then the Pacific. Only the very broadest ends and limits belong to the level of grand strategy, which is established at the highest level of executive authority. In our historical example, Roosevelt, Churchill, and Stalin set the grand strategy. In the case of the United States, Congress had authorized the president to do this by declaring war but did not itself participate in the development of the grand strategy except to be kept informed. For a church, grand strategy would correlate to its top level of missional, theological, and ethical commitments.

Strategy proper falls immediately underneath grand strategy, to create sweeping campaigns as the means to accomplish it. During the Second World War, top generals such as Eisenhower, MacArthur, Montgomery, and Vasilevsky formulated strategy. Examples of their strategic decisions include the deployment of more and better equipment to the European theater than to the Pacific until 1945; the timing and order of invasions in North Africa, Italy, and France; the scorched-earth defense along the eastern front; and the island-hopping offensive across the Pacific. In the church context, strategy might encompass far-ranging methodologies such as multiple services over larger buildings, church planting over multi-site expansion, or small group member care over pastoral visitation.

Operations are the largest building blocks of strategy. Operation Overlord was the code name for the Normandy invasion of June 1944. An operational decision is one that covers a complex plan that integrates a number of tactics and that achieves one of the major objectives needed to fulfill a strategy. A military decision at this level typically depends on

91

a team of generals, led by a commanding general, to develop and execute it. In the case of Operation Overlord, Eisenhower as Supreme Commander of Allied Forces in Europe was fully responsible for the operation. In fact, on D-Day he carried a sealed letter in his back pocket that he had written to be read only in the event of failure. Nevertheless, the senior military officers actually created the plans as a team, with Eisenhower's guidance. The analogy for a church might be a decision such as the launch of a new worship service, the start of a major global mission partnership, or the search for a new student ministries pastor.

Tactics are the various methods employed on the battlefield in order for the larger operation to succeed. Landing at Normandy instead of Calais was a tactic. The placement of inflatable rubber "tanks" in the phony camps of Patton's fictitious First U.S. Army Group to deceive Luftwaffe reconnaissance planes was a tactic. So was the use of Bangalore torpedoes to clear barbed-wire barriers above the landing beaches. The predawn paratroop drop to capture key bridges and road junctions just ahead of the landing was yet another tactic. These and many more were tactics in service of the same operation. Tactics in congregations encompass the inclusion of a five-minute faith story in every worship service, the security system for returning toddlers to the right parent, and the remodeling of a large classroom into a café to facilitate friendships with newcomers.

Using the fourfold breakdown of decision types above, how should the lead pastor be involved in each level? When a congregation values its senior pastor as the leader, it expects that the overall ministry will benefit from that leadership. But it also expects adequate accountability for the biggest decisions and sensible delegation of the smaller ones. How does that look in successful churches?

As the largest row of Table 8.2 depicts, the lead pastor does not typically formulate the grand strategy unilaterally, but certainly does lead the board through that critical process. This is one reason a Policy Governance model à la John Carver will not work well in a church setting without significant modification. Carver would have the board, of which the CEO is not a member, fully determine the ends and limitations policies—probably but not necessarily considering the CEO's suggestions—and only then hand them off to the CEO to implement as he or she sees fit. To cut the lead pastor out of defining the mission objectives of the church and out of drawing the borders of acceptable teaching and behavior is in no way compatible with setting up the pastor as the spiritual leader of the congregation.[6] The pastor of a large, thriving church, while constrained by policies to prevent a conflict of interest on performance and compensation, leads the board to accomplish its contribution to decision making at the grand-strategy level.

After leading the board to determine the grand strategy together, the pastor has a responsibility for leading the church as a whole to accomplish it. This responsibility requires a capable pastor to make strategic and major operational decisions with consideration of any and all wise input from board, staff, and resource people, but without any obligation to follow that input. Winning churches trust their lead pastor to hire and fire senior staff, start up and close down major ministries, and allocate many thousands of dollars to accomplish the mission and vision. If they can't safely extend that trust, they fix it by getting a new pastor who can do the job; it cannot be fixed by keeping an ineffective pastor tied up in red tape.

For operational decisions, the wise lead pastor stays engaged but learns to lean heavily on the senior staff team to come up with the right solutions and make them happen. As staff members demonstrate high capacity for effective independent action, the lead pastor can extend them more freedom to call the shots in their particular arena of ministry. For tactical decisions, the staff should be able to take the ball almost entirely after an adequate learning curve; if not, the lead pastor may do better to reassign them rather than overruling them.

The board decides the purposes and parameters

The move from small church to medium size typically involves a shift of emphasis from congregational decision making to board-level decision making. Churches that don't make at least that much of a shift never get out of first gear, and they stay small. If you want to talk about salaries and programming at church business meetings, you'll have a hard time attracting pastors who can lead their way out of a wet paper bag. What keeps medium-size churches from becoming high-impact ministries, however, is *not* making the shift from a board-led church to a staff-led church. The best way not to get stuck is to structure for the pastor to be the leader from the beginning. Nevertheless, the board plays a vital role in the majority of winning congregations.

In most cases the boards of thriving churches make the decisions at the grand-strategy level and offer counsel and support to the lead pastor for the strategy-level choices. As stated above, **the pastor leads the board through this process**. This happens by envisioning and inspiring the board, not by directing or controlling the board. The latter would be inconsistent with the board's responsibility to hold the lead pastor accountable.

Various models for board work are available. Some larger churches do not intentionally select a model or strategy but simply ease their way over the years into a rough approximation of a corporate business board. This may happen by default as a result of more, though not all, board members being selected from the ranks of business leaders. They do what they know to do. Reference has already been made to Carver's Policy Governance model, which is increasingly popular but requires modification for church use.[7] My Accountable Leadership strategy draws on the best of several models, including Carver, and assigns the board the specific role of governance, which is defined as (1) formulating the Guiding Principles, a grand-strategy document, (2) monitoring and supporting the lead pastor, and (3) fostering a vital connection with the church's Owner, Jesus Christ, and the people through whom his authority is entrusted to the board, as those people are understood according to the church's polity.[8] In Accountable Leadership, the board governs, the pastor leads, and the staff manages. The division of labor is based on the type of issue, not the magnitude.

Some boards of larger churches tend to make the division of labor by order of magnitude. This might be called a *macromanagement model* rather than a *governance model*. If the pastor and staff manage decisions that cost thousands of dollars, the board weighs in to manage when millions are involved. If the pastor and staff deal with segments of the church ministries and members, the board tries to manage only the decisions that affect everyone. This kind of criterion, however, becomes more and more unwieldy and arbitrary the larger the church becomes.

One very notable exception to the preponderance of grand-strategy boards is Saddleback Church, under Rick Warren. The bylaws of Saddleback provide for a traditional short list of major decisions to be voted on by the congregation (they could save a few dozen trees by opting for a raise of hands over paper ballots!). The grand-strategy group, however, is the Pastor's Management Team, composed of Pastor Warren and a small group of pastors selected by him. A board of trustees elected by the congregation is also in place; its one required task is to set the compensation for the pastors.[9] That requirement removes the conflict of financial interest from the otherwise fully pastor-led church.[10]

Regardless of whether the board of a winning church uses a governance model or a macromanagement model, the essential contribution that a good board makes is to work with the pastor to establish the grand strategy. This includes the mission outcomes, acceptable means to achieve them, and accountability for the lead pastor for satisfactory progress in those terms.

The staff decides the operations and tactics

Large churches typically have multiple paid staff members, generally one full-time equivalent per hundred in worship attendance. Very large churches, with between one thousand and two thousand in worship attendance, have larger staffs, of course, but tend to have fewer paid staff members per hundred attendees and higher expectations of each one. Three broad categories are pastoral staff, program staff, and support staff.

Although healthy congregations promote the biblical concept of ministry by every member of the body, the staff team, including accountable volunteer staff members, is critical for equipping, mobilizing, and supporting everyone in the church willing to serve.

So what part does the staff play in decision making? Refer to Table 8.2. With regard to grand strategy, staff members should only be invited to join the team if they are ready to buy into the grand strategy established by the board and lead pastor. Their best role is to accomplish and celebrate it, not to help formulate it. Strategy-level decisions are a different matter. These choices are the purview of the lead pastor, but a healthy relationship with the staff team will include the opportunity to offer input—even vigorous input—on these choices while fully respecting and supporting the pastor's final call. The next two decision types, however, define the essential contributions of the staff.

Operational decisions are best made by the lead pastor and staff as a team. Vibrant congregations march forward toward their vision through a series of major campaignlike initiatives. What is the next big thing on the horizon? A high-profile outreach event? A new worship service or campus? A building program? Strategic partnership with a church-multiplication movement on another continent? When these kinds of major operations are created and refined in the team setting, they energize and unify the people who set the tone for the entire church.

Tactical decisions may be coordinated at team meetings as needed, but they are normally managed by individual staff pastors and directors for their respective ministries. Each has a team of his or her own to lead. Depending on the nature of the tactic and the wiring of the staff person, it will be chosen personally, worked out by the ministry team together, or delegated to a team member closer to the front-line action.

Best practice demands that a paid staff be viewed as a proactive investment rather than a reactive expense. Mediocre churches do not seem to understand this concept and wait for financial surplus or a pressing need before adding anyone. The right staff person at the right time and in the right position, however, does not cost the congregation money. Certainly there will be start-up costs to create a new position, but an effective staff more than pays for itself in two ways. By growing the number of people who serve and give, it broadens the base of support. By growing each church member's relationship to Christ and his mission, it increases the provision emanating from that base. "For where your treasure is, there your heart will be also" (Matt. 6:21).

Clear expectations make a difference

When children act like parents and parents act like children, the result is a dysfunctional family. The roles of tribe, congregation, lead pastor, board, and staff in effective churches do not correspond to particular family roles. The lead pastor, for instance, is not the dad; nor is the tribe the rich uncle or poor cousin, and so on. Nevertheless, the dynamics of family systems theory can be observed in the cohesions and conflicts of congregational leadership.[11]

Healthy boundaries that clearly define important roles and expectations are necessary to a thriving ministry. Although great churches use different models, clarity and integrity of differentiated functions are a mark of excellence they have in common.

A lead pastor whose father-in-law lacks the organizational insight of Jethro may need to bring in consultants and coaches who won't provide either free advice or free babysitting. From one fresh perspective or another, however, pastors need the occasional "What you are doing is not good" to keep them from wearing out themselves and all the people around them.

SUMMARY AND PREVIEW

- *The tribe (denomination or movement) at its best provides reinforcement and resources for good decision making in a church.*

- *The congregation's essential contribution is consenting to the decision process and to the decision makers.*

- *The senior pastor leads the board and the staff to play their respective roles and personally provides the strategic direction of the church.*

- *The board defines grand strategy, that is, the purposes and parameters.*

- *Staff members plan major operations as a team and select tactics on their own.*

- *Clear roles and healthy boundaries help minimize dysfunction and conflict.*

Coming next, Chapter 9 presents fifteen common decisions that most churches face and offers best-practice ideas found among larger, growing congregations.

CHAPTER NINE

Best Practices for Typical Decisions

If I have seen further
it is by standing on the shoulders of Giants.
Sir Isaac Newton

MR. MIYAGI GOT HIS CARS WAXED AS WELL as a paint job on his house, his deck, and his fence. Daniel-San got an education in karate, in courage, and in mentorship. Eventually he got a vintage convertible too. But on that first confusing day all he learned was: "Wax on, right hand. Wax off, left hand. Wax on; wax off. Breathe in through nose, out through mouth. Wax on; wax off. Don't forget breathe, very important."

The old Okinawan master in the movie *The Karate Kid* used unorthodox methods to teach blocking and punching. His young student had agreed not to question, only to obey. Of course, the time came when he was allowed to ask questions so that he could learn even more. Daniel was willing to follow the pattern he was given. He had seen for himself that Mr. Miyagi was not an example of "those who cannot do, teach." He was the real thing. He was the best.

Although there is surely more than one way to make good decisions in congregational ministry, some practices show themselves to be counterproductive and others to be exemplary. The former, dysfunctions, will be cataloged in Chapter 10. The latter, best practices, are described in this chapter. We will cover a dozen types of decisions that most congregations face, either from time to time or on a regular basis. For each one a handful of best practices is offered for consideration.

1. Hiring the lead pastor

Go for the best. It would be hard to think of a single choice with greater implications for the future of a congregation than who its lead pastor will be. C. Peter Wagner, perhaps the best-known church-growth guru of the late twentieth century, was asked years ago in a large seminar if the success of Willow Creek Community Church near Chicago, and that of Saddleback Community Church near Los Angeles, was overblown. After all, Willow Creek wouldn't be what it was if it did not have Bill Hybels as its pastor, and Saddleback wouldn't be what it was if it did not have Rick Warren as its pastor. Wagner responded, "The point is, Willow Creek *does* have Bill Hybels, and Saddleback *does* have Rick Warren." No lead pastor is forever, but we want to develop, attract, and support the very best we can for as long as we can.

Let go of the past. In some congregations, the resignation, for one reason or another, of the former pastor most often creates the need to find a new lead pastor. It also comes about less frequently through retirement, dismissal, or death. In the United Methodist tribe, it comes from a new appointment. Cutting across any of these causes is the level of expectancy preceding a departure, which ranges from "obvious inevitability" on one end of the spectrum to "total shock" on the other. Veteran church leaders know that pastoral transitions leave some members sad, some mad, and some glad, aside from those who are not emotionally invested in the congregation. For those who are invested, a major loss occurs. If the pastor left without any pressure, part of the church family may experience a feeling of rejection: the pastor wanted to work with others more than he wanted to continue with them. If pressure was applied, the pastor and the pastor's family will have to struggle through similar feelings. Rejection is a powerful emotion. Grace, forgiveness, and acceptance will be needed to let go of the past.

Apply the big five. As for the future, regardless of the cause and the relative expectancy of the former pastor's departure, a critical vacancy results. It is especially critical for larger, growing churches because their progress depends on leadership. The objective is to identify and secure the best available person to lead the church forward.

Consider how the five big value choices already settled in a winning church would apply to the objective of finding a new lead pastor. If mission is to drive the agenda, the question becomes, What kind of lead pastor do we need to take us to the next level of making disciples and multiplying congregations? If Christ is the one to please, we understand that this mission is not our own but his. It must proceed with prayerful dependence on his presence and guidance. If we are committed to strengthening the leadership of the pastor, we'll need to find someone with a track record deserving of such trust and support. If we are cost-effective rather than penny wise and pound foolish, we will invest what is needed both in the process and in the person. And if we want to foster health and courage over people pleasing, we will establish appropriate ground rules and follow them with integrity.

Use a capable consultant. At the tactical level, the first challenge is how to figure out the best way to proceed. The person who knows the most about what to do has just left the building. One best practice for the board is to spend the money to secure competent outside consultation. If your congregation is part of a regional group of churches well known for growth and multiplication, you may have expert help in the form of a superintendent or bishop. Experience is common in these positions but expertise is rare, unfortunately. Most larger congregations can opt to obtain a consultation apart from or in addition to their denominational structure. In short, get help.

Appoint a strong interim pastor. Unless a preplanned succession is under way, the first advice a good consultant will likely offer is to hire a well-chosen interim senior pastor. Many churches are tempted to "cheap out" at this point and fill the pulpit with existing staff, volunteers, and outside speakers. Big mistake. What any significant congregation needs during transition is a steady hand on the helm and a trustworthy voice from the platform (i.e., with no conflict of interest such as becoming a candidate).

The ideal interim pastor is able to lead the church through its transition, just as a permanent pastor will lead the church following the transition. After the long tenure of a former pastor, a congregation has a very strong tendency to swing the pendulum by calling a new leader with different strengths, taking the strengths of its previous leader for granted. A couple of years into the new tenure, a damaging discontent typically follows when the old strengths are missed by direct comparison. A strong enough and long enough interim pastor can spare the church this kind of whiplash.

Tie the search to the board. Who should search for the lead pastor? Some tribes have a prescribed procedure already laid out, but if not, it is best that the board itself be the group to conduct this search, aided by outside expertise. Second best would be a subset of the board. Third choice would be a team the board appoints that includes several board members. Why is the board itself best? Because the typical search team woos a pastor with bright promises of opportunity and support and then evaporates on the day the new pastor arrives. If the board makes those commitments, the board will be there to make good on them.

Look for the right track record. What criteria are important for the search? Beyond the obvious minimums of good character, sound doctrine, and capable preaching, what is needed most is effective leadership. Since most churches are not thriving, experience in leadership is no indicator of effective leadership. It might even be a contra-indicator! There are three things to look for: track record, track record, and . . . location. No, it's track record again. Have the potential candidates led a congregation to the level just beyond your status quo? If so, they can probably—no guarantees—do it again with your congregation. If they have no direct track record, do they have an analogous track record? What have they led to a sizable success? Here's a hint for where to look: some of the likely prospects are not looking for a job; they are blooming where they are planted—but they might be transplantable. Other highly effective leaders are out looking for a job because their last church didn't want the change they were bringing.

With momentum, consider succession, but not otherwise. One best-practice option for highly effective churches with strong lead pastors is succession planned in advance. This is a terrible idea for a congregation or ministry that is not growing. The last thing such an organization needs is continuity! A troubled church will not become a good church by imposing the leadership instincts that didn't work before onto the next pastorate. However, a church that has serious positive momentum may well want to hire an associate pastor years ahead of an anticipated transition. There should still be a confirmation process when the time comes to step into the lead role. Succession may not be the best option even with positive momentum if the departing pastor has been a strong charismatic figure. A good interim pastor helps buffer the next permanent leader from sharp comparison with a notable predecessor.

Avoid conflicts of interest with interims and associates. Best practices for the process of selecting candidates revolve around following good criteria with integrity. For example, an interim pastor or preacher should normally be ineligible as a candidate to avoid a conflict of interest, and this should be public knowledge. An interim who seeks overtly or surreptitiously to be considered for the permanent role is like a therapist who dates his or her patient—it is an inappropriate boundary crossing. A special place of influence is being exploited. If a church intends to promote an existing associate to the senior role, but wants confirmation, it should be honest and label his or her interim ministry as a trial period so that the bias is acknowledged.

Tell the truth about the level of support. If a church requires a supermajority of its members to call or ratify the calling of a lead pastor, the vote of the first ballot should be reported to the candidate accurately. Some churches vote a second time "to make it unanimous," which, of course, it doesn't. Candidates deserve to know what they are getting into. If the congregation is divided on the candidate but highly unified otherwise, it probably isn't the right match. If the congregation had unity issues already, the right new leader will not be put off by a majority vote that is not overwhelming; it simply reflects the hard work that God is calling the new pastor to do.

2. Firing the lead pastor

Protect long tenure for effective pastors. Having covered the decision-making process for hiring a lead pastor above, it should be noted that effective churches rarely find themselves using it. Why not? Because a long tenure with an effective lead pastor is almost always required for sustained growth and health. The best churches rarely change their primary leader. One study of successful turnaround stories in the United States revealed that the churches that overcame decline or stagnation to experience growth had pastoral tenures ranging from seven to thirty-eight years. The average tenure in a national survey was only 3.6 years.[1]

The long-tenure characteristic does not apply equally to other pastoral or program staff, which may need to be readjusted more often as changing needs require. Nor does a long tenure by a lead pastor guarantee a congregation success. Some pastors carefully guard their paycheck, willing to preside over years of plateau and decline at the church's expense. A longer pastorate is a necessary, but not a sufficient, condition for sustained growth. The point here is that taking the action of dismissing or pushing out a senior pastor is costly to a church in many ways and should not be undertaken unless absolutely necessary.

Have a nondebatable reason. Winning churches do not push out a lead pastor on a judgment call to solve a power struggle or perception problem.[2] There are three nondebatable reasons for forcing the departure of a lead pastor: (1) major moral failure, (2) false teaching on essential doctrine, and (3) prolonged inability to accomplish the vision. The first violates God's love, the second violates God's truth, and the third—measured by growth over years rather than months—fails God's purpose. Any lesser reason for a forced departure amounts to someone's personal agenda for control and not to best practice for an excellent ministry. By contrast, a church that fails to dismiss a lead pastor for the reasons above is equally dysfunctional. That failure amounts to elevating a human personality above the integrity, identity, and mission of the church.

Tell the truth about the reason. With a nondebatable reason there is no need for disingenuous spin control beyond speaking the truth in love. Care should, of course, be taken not to share certain details that would create unnecessary harm. If the reason for pushing a lead pastor out is debatable, it is also insufficient, and no degree of spinning the story will change that.

Extend transitional support with impressive generosity. Leith Anderson has said at training events, "I believe in excessive severance. The reason I believe in excessive severance is that it's the cheapest way to go." When feelings are running high, there are high long-term costs created for the church by trying to save money at a wounded pastor's expense.

3. Developing property and buildings

Use rented space as much as possible. Saddleback is infamous for not putting down roots until it had more than ten thousand people in worship attendance. Wayne Cordeiro's main church campus in Honolulu is Farrington High School, and his network of fifty New Hope campuses covers the Pacific Rim from China to North America.[3] There comes a time for most churches—but not all churches—when building will advance their impact more than renting, but most attach their identity to a piece of dirt far too soon. The most influential churches in North America used theaters, schools, and warehouses for many years before settling down. Yet even now, they continue to extend and expand their outreach through multiple sites that are mostly rentals.

Design facilities as multipurpose to a point. Even not-so-winning churches got the idea a few decades ago that building a pricey single-purpose sanctuary to use one hour a week was not the best use of resources. Flexible facilities such as gymnatoriums are an important tool. Moveable chairs on flat floors with retractable platforms make it possible to go from dinner theater to basketball camps to worship celebration in short order. There is a limit to the multiuse concept, however. As a congregation grows, it may at times leverage its ministry best through the judicious use of space designed for a limited range of purposes.

Use multiple services and sites to expand proactively. When a growing church has reached 80 percent of its maximum capacity, it needs to find more. The options are: meet more times in the same space (schedule), enlarge the space (build), change to a bigger space (move), or add more spaces (branch). The last option is all the rage, and for good reason. If a church has an outstanding communicator, it makes sense to multiply venues with the same speaker with the help of technology. This may be temporary or a stepping-stone to church planting. Teaching teams are another option. Be sure to maintain a single vision, a single budget, and a single staff across the whole ministry, even if subdivided somewhat by campus. Otherwise, it's not a multisite church but a multiheaded nightmare.

Relieve one pinch point a time. Generally there are three kinds of spaces that need to match up: auditorium space, group (aka educational) space, and parking space. But don't match them up. How growing churches advance best is often by building what is needed and then fixing only the one type of space that is pinching worst. If parking is the biggest problem, fix only that. It will be easier to raise the limited funds for the one place where people are feeling the problem. This will allow some growth that sets up one of the other spaces as the next pinch point. Grow, pinch, fix, repeat. It's a little bit like walking. You push yourself off balance and catch yourself with the other leg—except in this case you have three legs.

Make prudent use of borrowed funds. It is great to pay with cash as much as possible. Maintaining little or no debt frees up space on the budget and adds extra peace of mind. But Larry Burkett was not the fourth member of the Trinity; and there is no prohibition in Scripture against borrowing when needed, only warnings about the consequences of excessive debt. Especially when interest is low, the amount is modest, and the need is urgent, don't hold ministry progress hostage to an ideal of zero debt. However, catch the qualifier *prudent* as well. Don't hold ministry hostage to a crushing obligation either.

4. Creating annual budgets

Fund the essential mission outcomes first. Cost-effectiveness is not always about bold spending. Sometimes it requires cutting the right expenses or reallocating them. Bayside—a fifteen-year-old church of more than ten thousand people near Sacramento, affiliated with the Evangelical Covenant Church—falls into the category that Lyle Schaller places beyond the megachurch: the "mini-denomination." Nevertheless, like most every organization during the economic recession of 2009, it had to make some hard budgetary choices. When the lead pastor, Ray Johnston, brought the first budget draft to his board, they noted that it saved money by putting their three mission priorities below the line (i.e., in the wish-list section of the budget if extra funds were available). The board sent the budget back and required that the priorities be funded above the line. Twenty-four staff members, mostly part-time, were laid off as a result.[4] It wasn't painless, but to do otherwise would have redefined *priority* to mean *option.*

Present the budget publicly in broad categories. Members with questions can be given access to unpublished budget details other than individual salaries upon request, but what they need to know as a group is the bottom line and the handful of components that create it. When I pastored a large church, the budget was broken down two different ways: by area of ministry (each of which required various kinds of expense) and by kind of expense (each of which went to various areas of ministry). Two pie charts depicted the breakdown of the whole from these two different perspectives. This level of detail gives members what they need to ratify an acceptable budget. Even if members don't vote on the budget officially, this information helps them support the ministry with confidence.

Rely on staff to create the budget. Governance boards set requirements for budgets and check them for compliance. Even a managing board in larger churches would only weigh in on a handful of broad numbers. Use the staff to formulate the budget, and hold the staff accountable by holding the lead pastor accountable.

Establish criteria in advance for an acceptable budget. When the typical church board reviews a proposed budget, each member applies his or her own standards to it. Does this look like something I would do in my business? Does this look like the budget at my cousin's church? Does this budget fund my pet projects? And so on. Excellent church boards, by contrast, develop and agree on clear criteria for what makes a budget acceptable and then apply those criteria to any budget under review. The right questions include: Does this budget fund our primary purposes? Does it avoid financial jeopardy? Does it take year-to-year trends into consideration? And so on.

Consider the option of leaving budget approval to the board. The congregation should see the broad strokes of the budget; otherwise it may compare its leadership unfavorably with that of most other organizations that publish their essential data. It makes little practical difference, however, whether a congregation actually casts a ballot on the budget. In either case, the details are established at leadership levels. If members were to vote down an annual budget, the issue would not be the budget at all but rather basic confidence in who the leaders are. That is the more meaningful decision for the members to make, depending on polity.

5. Staffing for success

Hire an executive pastor. Staffing configurations need to change with size—not the current size of the congregation, but the size it wants to be. Lead pastors of thriving churches with more than one thousand members almost invariably have one key associate who basically runs the place. This allows the lead pastor to concentrate more on excellent teaching, visionary leadership, and contributing to mission beyond the local level. Even small and middle-size congregations begin the executive role by using a volunteer or part-time pastor or administrator this way. Doing so provides short-term benefits and sets a congregation up strategically to break future growth barriers.

Supplement with part-time and contract staff. Especially with technology and new economic realities, churches can be as creative as necessary to get the help they need. Trying to innovate in a small town with little expertise available locally? Why not hire a coach or consultant one day a week to juice up board governance, pastoral leadership, and staff management by phone or online? Located in a city? There is an army of potential part-time staff available to you for various needs. And since your congregation is not their sole support, it is easier to make changes without high costs and emotions.

Invest in volunteer staff. Even the smallest congregations can organize for progress with a staff-led model by using volunteer staff. Large churches tend to pay all of their top ministry leaders but also treat volunteers like staff members to leverage the impact of the team. Investing in unpaid staff includes lavish appreciation, professional training events, great equipment, and ample clerical support.

Staff works for the lead pastor—period. Best practice is to keep accountability clean and simple: one team and one leader of that team. When staff members see that in practice their hiring, firing, or compensation are approved at the board or congregation level, they instinctively know that what they really must do is satisfy the majority of that group. Words on paper about being accountable to the pastor have little meaning under those conditions. Multiple lines of authority foster political tensions. The best practice whereby a board ensures fair treatment of staff is to require the lead pastor to follow a reasonable process but not enter into that process itself.

Evaluate performance with integrity, based on prearranged expectations. It's hard to score if the officials keep moving the goal during the game. Objectives and duties must be made clear up front and then actually used as the standard when it comes time to review performance. For this reason standardized evaluation tools can be misleading and even abusive if they are not fully customized to the stated requirements of the position. Consistent criteria are especially important—for the sake of integrity as well as legality—when an employee is asked to improve under a performance plan or probationary period.

Structure compensation strategically rather than conventionally. Congregations often get hung up on salary grids designed to replicate what other congregations are paying or what someone's idea of a comparable position in another organization is paying. Effective churches may devise grids of their own, but they think strategically rather than conventionally about compensation. That means paying what is needed (a) to attract an effective person, and (b) to keep him or her happy enough to stay. Paying more than that amount deprives the congregation of a larger staff. Paying less than that deprives the congregation of a better staff. The wrong staff person is never a bargain at any price.

Some tribes impose a grid that compensates productive and unproductive personnel equally. Under that regime, it becomes important to find creative ways other than salary to reward good work. Job retention, desirable assignments, professional development, good press, and outside opportunities all factor into the satisfaction of a lead pastor or a staff member.

6. Setting up the board

Keep a governance board small but not too small. The Evangelical Council for Financial Accountability requires a minimum of five board members. To that floor I would add nine as a maximum, but either five or seven would be optimum. All of these figures include the lead pastor in the count. An odd number is helpful for not risking deadlock. Three is generally legal and is good for agility, but is weak on accountability because the pastor only needs to convince one person. Seven is no better or worse than five as long as the congregation has capable volunteer leaders to spare. Nine is workable, though a few members will likely not engage as fully as the others. Any number in the double digits is likely to result in a board within a board dynamic as well as a senseless diversion of talent from ministries that need leaders in the staff realm.

Train and screen for agenda harmony. Diversity of background, skill set, and personality are beneficial to a board, but diversity of agenda is deadly.

No one should serve on the board who does not wholeheartedly support the theology, mission, vision, structure, and lead pastor of the congregation. Conflicted churches may entertain the notion that a devil's advocate or other counterweight to the pastor is beneficial on the board, but none of the best-practice churches referenced in this book think or act that way. Other than serious ethical or theological violations, the only reason for a board not to support a lead pastor is failure to lead the congregation to healthy growth over a reasonable period of time. A prerequisite training course taught by the lead pastor is a good way to prepare and check for a good fit.

Unify behind majority decisions. Agree on an appropriate simple majority or supermajority needed for key decisions and maintain a mutual commitment to stand in unity behind them. Group think is a common weakness of boards and is made worse by the subtle pressure for unanimity.

Guard against conflicts of interest. Best practice is not to allow staff members other than the lead pastor to serve on the board because it hinders the pastor's ability to hold them accountable. Relatives and business associates of staff also bring conflicts of interest. More subtle but also commonly damaging are board members who serve to champion the cause of a special-interest group within the congregation or an outside organization that stands to gain or lose from the board's decisions.

Keep terms of service short. Annual renewable terms provide the members of the board a chance to evaluate their service in the natural cycle of the ministry year. Also, if a board member does become a problem for the harmony and productivity of the group, an annual term provides a more gracious exit than a request to step down.

7. Managing programs

Make all programming decisions at the staff level. Effective large churches leave ministry operations to the pastor and staff. By contrast, a small congregation might hold long discussions from the floor before moving the worship service half an hour earlier or later. Middle-sized congregations might expect their board to ponder whether to launch a second service. In a church of thousands, however, both the congregation and the board would simply get an e-mail from the staff team to let them know what was coming. Consider the irony of smaller churches that think they need to hold on to control. The same kinds of changes in a megachurch affect many more people and dollars than they do in a smaller setting, but it is the smaller church that feels uneasy about trusting the pastor's team with decisions for change.

Control the quality of essential services. If a church has no lunch-hour Bible studies for business people during the week, newcomers to Sunday worship will not be put off. Just don't try to get by without a good nursery. There are at least half a dozen essential programs that people expect to be there when they walk in the door. If one of them is missing, the church will be perceived as having a major defect. Culture determines the exact list, but commonly it includes music, preaching, child care, children's programs, youth ministry, and classes or groups for adults. It may include others. Accountable staff, whether paid or volunteer, should manage such essentials with care for excellence.

Catalyze entrepreneurial outreach ministries. From a strong home base of essential services, an unlimited variety of ministries to the community can spring up. MOPS, Awana, Celebrate Recovery, Alpha, clothing drives, puppet teams, excursions for seniors—there is no end to the list of good ministries that church members can initiate and sustain. It is essential to have these kinds of targeted ministries but not essential to have any one of them in particular. Each one should be allowed to rise and fall with the vision and commitment of people who wish to lead and provide it. Best practice with these is for staff to offer them encouragement and a measure of support but not to take responsibility for their success or existence. Some minimum standards for the use of the congregation's good name also make sense.

Put leadership development first. Bill Easum relates that back when he served as the senior pastor of a large church, he eventually got to the point of asking for only one major goal from each staff member: how many new leaders are you going to create this year? Organized ministries will not be held back by a lack of people with needs or a lack of program materials on the market. It's all about raising up leaders, because leaders make things happen. Effective churches reflect this priority in how they spend time and money.

Attach every program to the Great Commission. If a church is focused outward instead of inward, every component of its operations should be asked this question: how does our team, department, and so on bring people to Christ? Sometimes it may be an obvious contribution, sometimes a supportive role, and sometimes a creative one. For example, a worship team obviously presents and supports the good news during services, but it might also take on performing or teaching out in the community to touch people not ready to visit a church. If a program does not contribute to the mission of the congregation, the program should either be changed or discontinued.

8. Maintaining bylaws

Fulfill outside mandates as flexibly as possible. Government regulations and denominational commitments will impose certain requirements. These must be honored, but not necessarily in the manner the bureaucrats in either realm prefer. Healthy churches do what they are required to do, and with integrity; but they also preserve as much freedom and flexibility for their own leaders as possible. Do not produce bylaws that build *a hedge around the law*, as the Pharisees did. If required to appoint some officer or committee that does not align with your chosen organizational strategy, do so and check the box on the form. Then be as creative as necessary either to adapt such elements to fit or else minimize them through benign neglect.

Differentiate the essential roles and functions cleanly. Whereas a denominational book of church order does not supersede them, the bylaws transmit a defined authorization from the church to the board and lead pastor.

The bylaws are normally the way to prescribe the purpose and selection of each essential position and group that make decisions in a process that has official sanction. Most decisions should be made at a single level, without multiple layers of approval. Those with heavy permanent consequences might require recommendation at one level and ratification at the next higher level. The best churches are careful to avoid conflicts of interest. For that reason, other than the lead pastor, who is rescued from any decisions of self-interest, no staff or their family members serve on the board.

Keep quorum and majority minimums easy to manage. A quorum of 10 percent or less is common for membership meetings in larger, growing congregations. Decisions are by simple majority except for a very few items such as calling or removing a lead pastor and amending the bylaws. Generally, two-thirds is sufficient for a supermajority in these cases. Requiring a supermajority has an upside and a downside. The upside is potentially to keep highly important choices from being controlled by a determined minority who might, for example, organize themselves to dominate a meeting not well attended by others as prepared as themselves. The downside is to risk the frustration of a majority of members who fail to achieve a supermajority and are forced to live with the choice of the minority.[5] For board meetings, a majority of its members is the usual quorum. Because of higher expectations placed on leaders, this quorum is not difficult to achieve, especially when participation by phone or Internet is allowed.

Mandate very few meetings. There is no good reason to require membership meetings more frequently than once a year. Special meetings can be called if needed. Likewise, it is not really necessary to mandate the meeting schedule of the board. Board members who can be trusted with the heavy decisions at that level can certainly be trusted with scheduling their work. A board must meet at least annually in order to function at all, of course. Two to four meetings each year are sufficient for a well-ordered governance board. Monthly board meetings are a long-standing tradition in churches of all sizes, but even these will prove insufficient for boards attempting to manage the finances and ministries of a church. Larger churches leave such work to the staff within parameters set by the board.

Keep bylaws concise. On the whole there is often an inverse relation-ship between the length of a church's bylaws and the rate of its growth. It is not cause and effect but rather two effects that are both caused by the level of confidence in pastoral leadership. Megachurches, with the occa-sional exception, have surprisingly short and simple documents. Peter Wagner used to say at his church-growth seminars in the 1980s that new churches should not buy any land or write any bylaws until they have at least five hundred people. The first limits vision and the second limits pastoral leadership when decided by smaller groups than that.

Constrain the contents of each organizational document to its neces-sary purpose. Documents that must be filed and government approved (e.g., articles of incorporation in the United States and both letters patent and bylaws in Canada) should be especially minimal without neglecting required mandates. Any further rules of the road that a church needs can be written into a lower level of policy document not subject to outside interference.

Do your homework. Short does not mean sloppy. When composing or amending organizational documents with legal implications, excellence requires research and outside review. For example, from a legal point of view, if a congregation is organized as a corporation in the United States, its authority is recognized as being vested in or delegated by the members of that corporation. The members of the corporation may or may not be the same set of people known as the "members of the church." Each state has its own laws as to the composition of statutory corporate membership. Depending on what these laws allow, possibilities for the corporation members may include all recorded church members, church members of a certain age or commitment level, the members of the board, or the board or corporation itself as the sole member. They might even be trustees from outside the congregation for caretaking or supervision.

There is a wide but limited range of legal options within which the ecclesiastical alternatives must fall—assuming the church wants to use a corporation to conduct its ministry.

Each of the legal options has advantages and disadvantages. A Baptist church in Nevada setting up its bylaws to define membership might do well to word them differently from the same kind of church in neighboring California. Why would that be? Nevada law allows a religious nonprofit corporation either to have or not to have statutory members, and it allows for persons to have voting rights without being defined as members by law. If the corporation does have members, Nevada mandates certain provisions that cannot be altered by the church through articles or bylaws, including a right to copy records and to sue the church for damages and legal fees if denied that right. So, if a church is located in Nevada, the option of no statutory members is the best way to allow the church to define its own membership concept without external mandates. California law, how-ever, defines a member as any person who has a right to vote on board members, corporate dissolution or merger, or disposition of all assets. So it is not possible to give people these voting rights without defining them as statutory members. Unlike Nevada, however, California allows the bylaws to define the specific prerogatives of membership without imposing mandates regarding matters such as copying records.[6]

Many things would be less boring than studying corporate law to the best advantage of a church's bylaws. One of them would be to find one's church in the middle of a lawsuit down the road. But most churches would find the tedium of doing their homework preferable to the excitement of litigating their neglect.

9. Managing membership

Create more than one commitment level. New Hope Church, under Pastor Wayne Cordeiro, is famous for getting new people to start serving on teams soon after they show up. Does your congregation have a way for newcomers to consider it "their church" even if they are still sorting out their faith? On the other end of the spectrum, leaders should meet the highest expectations, even beyond standard membership requirements. In between there is membership, but there might also be other options, such as signing up for a small group. Some congregations with built-in denominational distinctives add a type of associate membership or partnership for committed Christians who may not agree on some fine point of doctrine but who want to support the mission of the congregation in every way possible.[7]

Tie membership to active service expectations. Rapidly growing congregations normally have larger attendance numbers than membership numbers. Stagnant congregations with unpurged rolls have just the reverse. Best practice is to make membership mean something. Beyond a profession of faith and the appropriate evidence, members may be asked to give of their time, talent, and treasure, and to submit to the pastoral leadership. Each tribe and congregation will have its own standards, but membership is an ideal place to apply them.

Integrate joining the church into a web of on-demand growth opportunities. Saddleback has its 101, 201, 301, and 401 classes. Lyman Coleman, who developed Serendipity small group materials, used the metaphor of a subway system with a lot of stops and routes. Excellent congregations prepare resources and opportunities for each stage and facet of a person's spiritual journey, whether it is viewed as linear or unpredictable. Becoming a member is a rite of passage that should be intentionally related to spiritual preparation and spiritual follow-through. It is not an opportunity to be missed.

Keep membership meetings aligned with God's mission and good pastoral leadership. One regular business meeting annually is best at the membership level. Special-purpose meetings can be called as needed. The best annual meetings showcase ministry results, report the essentials of current conditions, and take a few simple up or down votes on necessary items that have previously been prepared, recommended, and explained. A majority decision at whatever standard has been set in the bylaws is just as valid as a unanimous vote. Calls to wait for unanimity, often by those who desire a veto for their minority view, should be resisted. A commitment to unity and integrity means expressing different views candidly and then mutually supporting decisions that are made by a process to which every member agreed when he or she joined.

10. Exercising church discipline

Consider the option of renewable church membership. First Baptist Church of Clovis, for example, requires members to recommit each year.[8] This prompts self-examination and self-screening prior to any need for intervention. When a problem situation does emerge, the annual check makes it easier to discover and address. If necessary, an application to rejoin can be declined. This puts church discipline on a more positive footing.

Invest generously in those who come clean. Everyone has struggles, and no one enjoys shame. When someone has failed in a way that damages family and congregation, it is common to find correction met with denial and defensiveness. When an offender is genuinely sorry and willing to submit to a process of repentance and restitution, excellent congregations respond with grace and practical assistance.

Protect the church decisively from those who resist correction. Healthy churches do not accommodate dysfunction. When grace and truth are presented and resisted, a priority on protecting the rest of the flock requires removal from membership and participation. This step is tough love, in the hope that the offender will at some point recognize his or her problem and seek help for it. In the meantime, the congregation remains a safe and nurturing place for the benefit of others.

11. Starting congregations

Combine multisite expansion and church planting. Healthy disciples reproduce disciples. Healthy leaders reproduce leaders. Healthy churches reproduce churches. New congregations may be started internally or externally. Starting satellite congregations that remain under the wing of the sponsoring church is not new, but it is a strong new trend. The best practice is to combine multisite expansion and church-planting multiplication. Each has its advantages, and together the two strategies can complement each other. For example, New Hope transitions its new congregations from video venues of Wayne Cordeiro to campus pastors under his supervision to separate but affiliated churches.

Reproduce at a bold but sustainable rate. Larger churches that wish to make a Kingdom impact that continues beyond themselves become multiplying churches. This requires commitment and generosity but not too much sacrifice. It is far better practice for a sponsoring congregation to spin off 10 percent of its people every three years than to send 25 percent out once and never do it again.

Reproduce multipliers, not just mules. Great investors take advantage of compound interest to multiply their returns in the market. Reproducing new congregations that reproduce others is the compound interest of the Kingdom. If your church is going to go to the effort to start others, best practice is making sure the visionary DNA to do the same is passed on to each generation. Many church plants are like mules, which are strong but cannot reproduce.

12. Choosing mission partners

Go where the fish are biting. Doors open and close in God's providence at different times around the world. The mandate to make disciples of every ethnicity requires that any culture with no availability of the gospel at all must be identified and given a high priority. In addition, since God is "no respecter of persons," as the King James Version puts it, in cultures that do have the gospel, those with the greatest receptivity—whether across the street or across the globe—deserve the highest investment. In their local outreach winning churches go where the fish are biting, and instinctively seek the ripest harvest abroad as well.

Combine a shotgun approach and a rifle approach. The Great Commission is global, but even a large congregation cannot engage in every type of ministry to every tongue and tribe. What often works best is a combination analogous to the old over-and-under gun that normally combined a rifle barrel on top of a shotgun barrel. Any healthy, growing church can make a significant contribution to world mission by concentrating its resources and personal efforts on one or a few carefully selected fields. This rifle approach also creates a deep experience of partnership between the sending church and its partnering church or ministry on the ground. However, each congregation has a responsibility to equip all of its members to fulfill their God-given calling to advance the gospel around the world. The leading of this or that individual member may not line up with the mission-rifle partnership of his or her church. For that reason it is healthy for congregations to maintain some kind of shotgun approach whereby any member who God leads to international ministry can receive some measure of encouragement and support from his or her home church.

Choose partnerships that work in the twenty-first century. Texans have a colorful expression: "He's all hat and no cattle." Winning churches place high expectations on their own fruitfulness and on those people and organizations they select as partners. Sadly, many mission organizations that innovated and made their mark in the last century have not maintained their edge in recent decades. They have adopted new buzzwords and bits of technology but still rely on traditional strategies that are high cost and low impact. Large missional churches are doing more direct global ministry on their own and contracting specialized expertise as needed. Information on the status of unreached people groups and on the financial practices of mission organizations is readily available.[9] It is more challenging to evaluate the cost-effectiveness of one organization over another compared with a do-it-yourself approach.

SUMMARY AND PREVIEW

Best practices are worth following in these areas:[10]

- *Hiring the lead pastor*
- *Firing the lead pastor*

- *Developing property and buildings*

- *Creating annual budgets*

- *Staffing for success*

- *Setting up the board*

- *Managing programs*

- *Maintaining bylaws*

- *Managing membership*

- *Exercising church discipline*

- *Starting congregations*

- *Choosing mission partners*

As the flip side of best practices, the final chapter of *Fish or Cut Bait* is a catalog of dysfunctions to avoid. A top ten list appears for each of five levels: congregation, board, pastor, staff, and tribe.

CHAPTER TEN

A Catalog of Dysfunctions to Avoid

*There is a deep fundamental dysfunction
in the way we gather intelligence and
provide information to the decision makers.*
John Lehman, 9/11 Commission

THE OPENING SCENE OF THE MOVIE *Cold Mountain* depicts a historical event from the American Civil War, namely, the Battle of the Crater in 1864. An explosion rips the earth apart underneath fortifications surrounding the Confederate stronghold at Petersburg, Virginia. The Union troops pour through the breach in the defenses and expect to win an overwhelming victory. Instead, they are slaughtered. Something went wrong.

Let's rewind the reel to a point before the movie begins in order to understand what happened that July 30 in 1864. The war was well into its fourth and final year, but the Southern capital of Richmond was still in Rebel hands. Before it could fall, the railway supply center of nearby Petersburg had to be taken. Unfortunately for the Yankees, it was heavily fortified with a series of trenches and bulwarks. The siege began on June 15.

A mining engineer in civilian life, Lt. Col. Henry Pleasants of the 48th Pennsylvania Infantry suggested a novel plan to end the siege and take the city by direct force. He proposed digging a T-shaped mine shaft to begin fifty feet below the Confederate defenses, out of their line of sight. It would run more than five hundred feet to reach the line and then split both left and right directly parallel and twenty feet beneath it. The top of the T would be packed with gunpowder and detonated. This would kill the defenders in the area and open a breach in the fortifications at the same time. Maj. Gen. Ambrose Burnside approved the plan.

The shaft was completed successfully. The top of the T, seventy-five feet in length, was packed with 320 kegs of gunpowder, for a total of eight thousand pounds. For two weeks prior, a division of black Union soldiers under Brig. Gen. Edward Ferrero was intensively trained in a precision maneuver to exploit the breach in two brigades, one to the left of the crater and the other to the right. It was all set. Superior numbers, the element of surprise, overwhelming firepower, meticulous training—nothing had been overlooked, except, of course, a last-minute leadership dysfunction.

Burnside's superior, Maj. Gen. George Meade, had misgivings about the plan and ordered Burnside to replace the black division with a white one. Meade was afraid that if the black troops failed and suffered high casualties, the top brass would be taken to task in the Northern newspapers. Burnside appealed to Meade's superior, Lt. Gen. Ulysses S. Grant, but Grant backed Meade. Burnside had no choice but to replace the highly trained black division. When no white division volunteered for the last-minute switch, their commanders drew straws. Brig. Gen. James Ledlie lost the draw and gave his brigade commanders vague instructions before retiring to his tent.

Shortly before 5:00 a.m. on July 30 the ground shook with the force of the largest man-made explosion to date on the North American continent. About three hundred Confederates were killed instantly, and a crater opened some 170 feet long, 100 to 120 feet wide, and 30 feet deep. Into the breach ambled Ledlie's division; the good colonel himself lay drunk in his tent behind the lines. The only problems were that they had waited for ten minutes before starting out, they moved slowly, and instead of skirting the edges of the crater as the original division had been trained to do, Ledlie's men entered the crater itself, thinking it might make good cover. They were wrong about that. They were trapped against walls of the crater as tall as a three-story building. Meanwhile, the surviving Confederates had regrouped and now ringed the edge of the crater with their muskets pointing down toward the sea of blue uniforms thirty feet below. When Burnside heard of the fiasco, instead of withdrawing the white division, he sent the black division into the crater to help them. Both Union divisions were cut down by merciless musket fire in a death trap of their own ingenuity. The Southern commander on the scene, Brig. Gen. William Mahone, later described it as a "turkey shoot."

Politics at the leadership level snatched defeat from the jaws of victory. But that would never happen in the church, would it?

Larger, growing congregations face and overcome many problems, but they were only able to develop into larger, growing congregations by learning to avoid or eliminate a host of decision-making dysfunctions that characterize stagnant and declining ministries. Now that we've covered right answers to the big questions in Part 1, and the clear roles and best practices of winning churches in Part 2, let's consider a little catalog of dysfunctions that impede the ability of troubled congregations to make good decisions. For each of the five roles discussed in Chapter 8, a top ten list of "don'ts" is here offered to red-flag potential hazards that better churches avoid.

Disclaimers:

- *Some of the following dysfunctions will only pertain to one tribe or another, but most of them are equal-opportunity foibles.*

- *The lists are not presented in any order of importance and are suggestive rather than exhaustive.*

- *The summary for this final chapter will be in the form of a table in the conclusion.*

Top ten dysfunctions at the congregation level

1. Maintain confusing, overly detailed bylaws.

One church I assessed had bylaws to choke a horse. Page after page strove to legislate for every conceivable contingency. One good sentence I discovered was the following: "The pastor is the leader of the church."

When I reported to the congregation, I said, "Your bylaws really only say two things: (1) the pastor is the leader, and (2) just kidding."

2. Acquiesce to a big donor's questionable agenda.

It happens all the time. Although those who give generously should be appreciated, those who use their checkbook to manipulate a ministry are not giving at all. Instead, they are paying—and they expect something in return. God does not need their money, and neither does his church.

3. Use parliamentary procedure as the dominant feature of congregational meetings.

After Civil War general Henry Robert lost control of a congregational meeting, he vowed to master parliamentary procedure. His classic *Rules of Order* does help tame the chaos of floor fights. Effective churches, however, steer clear of pure democracy. It distracts from mission, weakens leadership, and accommodates controlling personalities.

4. Hold out for unanimity rather than unifying behind majority decisions.

Unity is not unanimity. The first is a commitment; the second is a circumstance. True unanimity—everyone holding exactly the same point of view—is rare. Holding up a decision until a display of "unanimity" is obtained is dysfunctional because it pressures some into joining the herd and grants others a veto.

5. Maintain low expectations of leaders.

Too often church members are quick to rationalize or spiritualize poor conditions and poor results. The flipside of trusting leadership to the pastor and governance to the board is expecting fruitfulness and integrity in return. Struggling churches attract and retain mediocre leaders in part because they expect so little from them and entrust so little to them.

6. Discuss sensitive details at the congregational level.

Life is lived in a fishbowl for the families of ministry staff. To some degree this is unavoidable. Churches that make personal details, such as individual salaries, public, however, add unnecessary pressure to these families. Choosing competent board members with no conflict of interest to oversee sound compensation policy is adequate for accountability purposes.

7. *Process difficult decisions in a single extended meeting.*

A decision that raises concern should not be proposed, discussed, and decided in a single meeting unless it is a true emergency. Healthy practice involves leadership recommendations, advance communications, and often a preliminary information meeting free of the pressure to make a decision on the spot. This process can later be followed with a simple up or down vote after members have had time to consider what they are doing.

8. *Give way to emotionally controlling personalities.*

Especially in a vacuum of firm spiritual leadership, congregations often fall prey to the personal agendas of individuals who use emotion, relationship, and loaded language to manipulate others. When a leadership crisis erupts, it does not take many tears and spiritual tones to tip a vulnerable congregation.

9. *Tolerate passive-aggressive behavior.*

Jesus said: "All you need to say is simply 'Yes' or 'No'; anything beyond this comes from the evil one" (Matt. 5:37). Unhealthy congregations, by contrast, allow influencers to combine nice talk or other language games with sabotage. Perceptive individuals know to ask no-nonsense questions that bring issues into the sunshine.

10. *Promote a "checks and balances" mind-set.*

Holding leaders accountable is one thing. Holding them back with red tape is another. Congregations that have been burned in the past try in vain to insulate themselves from potentially bad leaders by withholding authority from them. A lack of trust can only be solved by experiencing good leaders who are allowed to lead.

Top ten dysfunctions at the board level

1. Fail to screen for conflicts of interest.

Churches that let staff members and their immediate family on the board are asking for trouble. Board members too close to special interests inside the congregation or related to it also bring conflicts of interest. Unhealthy boards also fail to ask the lead pastor—who must be on the board—to step away from decisions when self-interest arises.

2. Confuse biblical titles with functional assignments.

Some churches think they have to put all their pastors on a board of elders because they've been told that "pastors" and "elders" are synonymous in the New Testament. One church that had "ministry coordinators" was told it was not fully biblical because it didn't have "deacons." This kind of confusion results from inadequate exegesis of the text and inappropriate application to a modern setting. Leaders in the same biblical category can serve with a variety of titles, assignments, and structures.

3. Treat stakeholders as if they were owners.

All owners are stakeholders but most stakeholders are not owners. Boards should consider their impact on significant stakeholders such as attendees, members, staff, related ministries, vendors, and so on, but they should take their agenda only from ownership. When they do otherwise, the ministry suffers at the very hands trusted to protect and promote it.[1]

4. Defer to "expertise" over agreed standards.

It is not uncommon for a board to have one or another member who is perceived to bring exceptional expertise in governance or finances. Dysfunction results when that member's own standards are substituted in practice for those agreed upon by the board and lead pastor.

5. Allow a vacuum in the office of lead pastor.

A vacuum is created when a lead pastor departs and the board inserts for the interim either no one or anyone other than another lead pastor.

Either to save money or to scratch someone's itch, the board may try to oversee the staff team itself or use an existing staff member. Any alternative to a capable interim pastor or a predetermined successor will alter the balance of power, with unintended consequences.

6. *Allow more than one line of accountability from staff.*

When a board member or the board itself deals directly with staff members on ministry issues, the senior pastor's leadership is compromised to one degree or another. How can the pastor deal firmly with an associate who connects with the board? How is it fair to hold the pastor accountable for staff results if the board is interfering? Multiple lines lead to confusion at best and division at worst.

7. *Triangulate information under the guise of protection.*

Board members who get mixed up in power struggles find any number of loopholes to the kind of direct resolution required by Scripture.[2] When you hear, "People are saying . . ." or "I promised not to say who told me this but . . . ," you know they are pursuing an unhealthy agenda of their own or facilitating one for someone else. *Triangulation* is the name of this dysfunction in family systems theory.

8. *Set financial limits too low or too high.*

Economies vary but some boards fail to identify an appropriate order of magnitude for financial controls. Those who neglect amounts that could put the church in jeopardy are not doing their job. Those who interfere with amounts used routinely in operations are doing the staff's job.

9. *Engage with employee and "customer" complaints.*

Some pastors have to contend with boards that are willing to allow in board discussions complaints from parishioners, staff members, or their surrogates. For a governance board this is completely out of bounds.[3] Even a smaller church using a management model would do well to point people with grievances directly to the person with whom they have an issue.

10. Use consultants to deflect responsibility.

Consultants, like chemical compounds, have different effects and different levels of potency. The right one at the right time for the right reason is a gift from God. When a board chair brings in a consultant as a wedge between the board and the lead pastor, however, the resulting dysfunction is similar to undue deference to an expert member of the board. "We had no choice, the consultant said . . ." This defense is not the sign of a responsible board.

Top ten dysfunctions at the lead pastor level

1. Pay too much or too little attention to precedent.

"Past performance is not a guide to future results." That disclaimer is printed on the cover of the typical financial prospectus. Smart investors read the prospectus anyway. Pastors who always follow the herd on the latest program need the *disclaimer*: "Just because it worked someplace else doesn't mean it will work for you." Pastors who always reinvent the wheel need the *prospectus*: "Just because you're smart doesn't mean you are smarter than everyone who already tried this."

2. Gloss over difficult problems.

While it is good to be positive whenever possible, some pastors put on a happy face when a hard question might be the better spiritual medicine. One reason that smaller and conflicted congregations cannot free themselves of dysfunctional patterns is that the person who should be leading them is too busy handing out lollipops.

3. Conflate first-century practice with biblical teaching.

God's people want to know that their decision making is either required or allowed by the Scriptures. Many pastors, however, mislead people by failing to distinguish the teachings of the New Testament from ancient or modern methods. The synagogue, for example, occurs in the New Testament but is not commanded. *Elders* and *bishops* are New Testament terms, but the elder board and the diocese are later inventions.

4. Treat staff with a "neglect and zap" approach.

Staff team members need to be managed in different ways, but they all need something from their boss in order to be happy and productive. Sometimes a lead pastor or an executive pastor acting as chief of staff disengages from the team and assumes that the team knows what is expected and that it has what it needs. Then, when the desired outcome fails to appear, the pastor reacts. This pattern is neither fair nor effective.[4]

5. Misuse development tools as evaluation tools.

Instead of using prearranged goals and expectations, some supervisors resort to standardized tools. This practice is abusive to staff and self-defeating for the organization. The proper use of such tools is the positive development of staff through personal insight in a safe context. Especially egregious is the misuse of a 360-degree evaluation, which becomes a weapon when used for review rather than for development.[5]

6. Assume an entitlement mentality.

Pastors who experience a measure of success sometimes develop a mentality that wraps the congregation around the pastors' own ego. The same malady of self-centeredness is found in another form among pastors of small, stagnant congregations. These pastors hunker down in a bunker of remnant theology and protect their rice bowl like the last of the truly faithful. Healthy pastoral leaders value the mission of the church above their own job security and perquisites.

7. Put idealism ahead of pragmatism.

A friend of mine, Jim Griffith, likes to admonish new church planters not to get themselves "drunk at the vision bar."[6] Because pastors ponder the eternal and dream big dreams for their congregations, they can operate on unrealistic expectations. Culture, economics, and imperfect people in a disappointing world[7] all factor into ministry in the real world. Envision what could be, but then get real and find something that works.

8. Put pragmatism ahead of integrity.

The Apostle Paul expressed a holy pragmatism for God's mission when he wrote, "I have become all things to all people so that by all possible means I might save some" (1 Cor. 9:22). Success for its own sake, however, leads some pastors to act without integrity; for example, by saying one thing and doing another just to get results.

9. Succumb to paralysis by analysis.

An excess of caution for fear of making a mistake keeps some pastors from making a decision. Many pastors are afraid that leading decisively will be viewed as inconsistent with servant leadership, as if the ultimate example of such a leader, Jesus, floated about harmlessly making suggestions. Jesus modeled decisive strength used for the benefit of others.

10. Fail to perform due diligence.

The opposite of excessive caution is inadequate caution. Pastors sometimes commit their ministries to a risky direction on a wing and a prayer. One way this happens to congregations is by taking on an imprudent level of debt. Another way it happens is by appointing leaders or workers without knowing their history.

Top ten dysfunctions at the staff level

1. Fail to develop a winning team together.

Patrick Lencioni suggests that the five dysfunctions of poor teamwork are absence of trust, fear of conflict, lack of commitment, avoidance of accountability, and inattention to results.[8] Church staff members need not be best friends or sing "Kumbaya," but they must deliver—and help one another deliver—the same vision.

2. Angle for multiple or fuzzy lines of accountability.

When lines of accountability are not clear and singular, no one is quite sure where to get direction. Sometimes associate pastors in particular want a direct line to the board even if their accountability on paper is to the lead pastor. Multiple lines to the board, however, set up political struggles that end badly for everyone.

3. Fail to clarify expectations of performance.

Some staff members make the mistake of thinking that their job security is better when expectations are unstated or unclear. That assumption, however, leads to festering dissatisfaction that erupts unpredictably. Just as students are more at ease when they know what will be on the test, healthy staff members benefit from clear goals and duties that they know will form the basis of their review.

4. Move the goalposts during an evaluation.

Whether instigated by a subordinate or a supervisor, it is inappropriate to change the criteria for evaluation after the performance to be reviewed is under way or completed. It is not fair to the employee or to the organization. Moving the goalposts during a probationary process is even worse.

5. Work an agenda out of synch with the pastor's vision.

Staff members should have freedom to dream and to lead with joy in their own scope of ministry. It is vital, however, that those dreams and leadership agendas contribute to the achievement of the lead pastor's vision rather than distract from or undermine it; otherwise, the staff member is not truly on the pastor's team in spirit and should not remain on it in body.

6. Act like an expense rather than an investment.

Staff members who fail to grasp their own value to the church may fail to grasp their need to live up to it. Mediocre congregations look at staff as a necessary expense in response to a need that can no longer be neglected. Proactive congregations invest in staff ahead of needs in order to create growth. Great staff members understand that they must pay for themselves in the long run, if not earlier.

7. Triangulate with influencers.

Misunderstandings, disappointments, and conflicts happen. The dysfunctional way to handle them is to spread them to third parties. This is called *triangulation*, or if two syllables are better than five, *gossip*. When a staff member meets with a board member or a generous giver for a burger with a side of grievance, healthy boundaries are being violated as well as biblical principles. There is no safe substitute for direct resolution with a supervisor.

8. *Fail to give and receive affirmation.*

People do work but are not machines. They need and deserve positive feedback for what they are doing right. When people are uncomfortable or unappreciated in their environment, they move on or cause problems. Wise leaders find out what their people need and give it to them. Wise teammates find ways to do likewise for one another.

9. *Give more attention to weaknesses than to strengths.*

Overly self-conscious leaders play into unrealistic expectations that congregations place on them to have every desirable trait. When a weakness becomes apparent, they allow it to become their focus until it is fixed. By contrast, effective leaders play to their strengths and help others do the same according to the gifts that God has given them.[9]

10. *Neglect the needs and relationships of spouses.*

When two are one flesh, the wounds of one leave scars on the other. The spouses of lead pastors and senior staff members have a palpable effect on the cohesiveness of the team, the results of its ministry, and the morale of the congregation. A spouse may need support to repair a relationship at home or with another staff family. The lead pastor, staff members, and congregation neglect these spouses to everyone's detriment.[10]

Top ten dysfunctions at the tribe level

1. *Pursue institutional aims over missional aims.*

Whether it's a denominational hierarchy or a voluntary fellowship, tribal entities wind up putting their own survival ahead of accomplishing mission—and they are very adept at insisting just the opposite. One way this shows up, for example, is with denominational executives who will not protect the back of a lead pastor trying to lead healthy change. Why not? There is a risk of losing financial support if the old guard prevails.

2. Underestimate the potential of franchising.

Are denominations dying or alive and well? The answer is yes. Old-fashioned loyalty to one's tribe of origin (once a Baptist, always a Baptist) is rapidly fading; but movements that flourish now also have brand names and features. "Yeah, we visited a Northpoint church; it was great." Existing denominations overlook the potential they have to reinvent themselves and develop a brand that can be scaled.

3. Keep the champions on the sidelines.

When most congregations in an association are idling or declining and its officials have never led a large church, the highly fruitful pastors in the group are made to feel out of place. They are too threatening. So they stay on the fringes and don't take the lead in tribal direction. Besides, they are busy with the thriving ministry of their congregation and find the tribe offers them little help. A few wise tribes learn to reverse this and make heroes and mentors of their best pastors.

4. Throw out the baby with the bathwater.

Each tribe has natural strengths that may be lying dormant. If it reinvents itself to leave all tradition behind, it might discard its best relationship or value-adding feature. One renewal organization decided to give up on its denomination completely and reorganize as a generic church-resource ministry. Unfortunately, it gave up the unique tie it had to its natural constituents, and many of them declined to join the new thing.

5. Stick with the good old boy network.

When organizations become ingrown, there is no way to stay healthy. Fresh blood helps the sick and injured get better. Fresh family members help the gene pool prevent birth defects. Tribes that keep recruiting for leadership roles from the same old members of the club need to be told that family reunions are not the best place to meet girls and boys.

6. Ignore the big financial trends.

The current economy, demographic trends, and global patterns affect tribal resources. When a denomination spends most of its time looking in the rearview mirror and trying to relive its glory days, it may miss the upcoming opportunity and hit the oncoming train instead.

7. Confuse the word denomination *with its reality.*

Some tribes deny being a "denomination." The tribe may want to seem new instead of old, voluntary instead of hierarchical, of God rather than of man. Whatever the motive, the denial obscures the reality that *to denominate* simply means to give a group a name. A set of congregations that have a connection to one another by doctrine, history, schools, or mission work is a denomination in practice. Missing that fact leads to missing others.

8. Place pastors with little regard to their track record.

Although it's no guarantee, the best evidence for what a person can do in the future is what he or she has done in the past. Denominations and other agencies that fail to ascertain and communicate pastors' previous achievements (not experience) do their congregations a disservice.

9. Fail to let pastors prove themselves.

This dysfunction is the flip side to the previous one. No one can develop a track record until they get on the track. Internships at winning congregations (why learn from those who do poorly?), behavioral leadership assessments, and campus pastor assignments (in multisite churches) are examples of stepping-stones.

10. Preserve strangleholds of historical polity.

Polity was created from biblical interpretation and historical experience. No one need disobey the Scriptures to make better decisions, but complex regulations can smother the life out of innovative leadership. Top denominational officials should simplify and eliminate regulations when possible. Further down the food chain, district and local leaders should explore all the options to adapt or minimize mandates to get the best results.

SUMMARY AND PREVIEW

The conclusion, coming next, includes a summary table of the catalog of dysfunctions.

Conclusion

Those are my principles,
and if you don't like them . . . well, I have others.
Groucho Marx

PICKING GREAT COMPANIES IS RISKY BUSINESS. Most of the eleven corporations that Jim Collins singled out in *Good to Great* are still going strong,
but Circuit City went bankrupt and Fannie Mae went to the U.S. tax-
payer for a nine-figure bailout.[1] Picking great congregations is tricky as
well. Those named in *Fish or Cut Bait* as winning churches are well
deserving of study and emulation, but there is no guarantee that they will
always follow right values and make good decisions years from now.

One megachurch in Georgia that I had originally thought to include
in my core group of ten winning congregations had to be cut from the list.
Within its first ten years it grew to more than five thousand in worship
attendance on a spacious hilltop campus at a strategic location. I recall
driving by and thinking, "Lord, who is this pastor to you that you would
give him a spot like that?!" In recent years, however, the church over-
reached on financing new buildings and then suffered a decline in
attendance as their heavy debt combined with a bad economy. They will
probably turn the corner at some point, but they can't be held up as a
model of great decision making for the present.

Even the best and brightest can make big mistakes. Lest we criticize
them too harshly, however, keep in mind that most of the congregations
in North America are stagnant or declining. Not many bother to critique
the majority because not much is going on there to start with. Although
no church is perfect, there are some notable islands of health in the sea
of dysfunction. Hopefully our exploration of how effective congregations

137

think and act has left you with some important questions to ponder and some helpful practices to consider.

Let's condense and integrate the major points of the book as we wind down. Then we'll close with a final caveat.

Encore presentation

First, what is it that makes for a "winning church"? We suggested three very simple criteria in the introduction.

TABLE 11.1—THREE CRITERIA OF A WINNING CHURCH

Criterion	Its Effect	Or Imagine Acts without It
God's Word	Biblical Integrity	And the disciples were filled with spiritual power and kept making disciples, and they all believed whatever they wanted to believe.
God's Spirit	Spiritual Vitality	And there were more disciples learning more of the apostles' teaching, and they were exactly the same as they had been before.
God's Mission	Missional Accountability	And the disciples worshiped with joy and taught the word with excellence, and when the twelve of them died it was all over.

If the people of a congregation hold true to the revealed truth of Christ in the Scriptures, if they consciously seek leading of the Holy Spirit in humble dependence, if they place the redemptive mission of God ahead of serving their own personal needs, then they bear the marks of the vibrant primitive church. They are a winning congregation that will glorify the Father by bearing much fruit.

Part 1 of the book dealt with the fundamental value choices that winning churches make differently than others do. We introduced the big five questions. Table 11.2 repeats the review presented in Chapter 7.

All good decision making begins with agreement on the very purpose a congregation has to exist. What is it that *must* be done? Winning churches are committed to God's plan for those who don't yet know him. How do we know that is the right answer? Who says so? Christ does, as the Lord and "Owner" of the church. Next we need to know who will take the lead. Large, thriving churches have strong lead pastors. What's all this going to cost? The simple answer: whatever it takes. Cost-effectiveness is more important than low price. What do we do when trouble comes? Courageous leaders speak the truth in love to dysfunction.

TABLE 11.2—THE BIG FIVE, ONE LAST TIME

Value Question	Winning Answer	Competing Answer
#1: What must be done?	Make new disciples	Serve the members
#2: Who says so?	Christ, the Owner	Influential stakeholders
#3: Who takes the lead?	The lead pastor	Influential board members
#4: What's it going to cost?	Whatever it takes	As little as possible
#5: What if there's trouble?	Speak truth in love	Speak inoffensively

Chapter 8 dealt with decision-making roles at five different levels. Table 11.3 contains them.

TABLE 11.3—DECISION-MAKING ROLES
IN WINNING CHURCHES

Role	Essential Contributions	Level	Verb
Congregation	Consents to decision-making process Consents to lead pastor and board	Support	Legitimize
Lead Pastor	Leads board to decide grand strategy Makes strategic decisions Leads staff to decide operations Leads congregation to support vision Represents congregation to tribe	Strategy	Lead
Board	Makes mission and boundary decisions Monitors performance of lead pastor	Grand Strategy	Govern
Staff	Makes operational decisions as a team Makes and delegates tactical decisions	Operations and Tactics	Manage
Tribe	Endorses the lead pastor and church Provides resources to the lead pastor and board	Reinforcement	Consult

TABLE 11.4—BEST PRACTICES AT A GLANCE

Hiring the lead pastor	Go for the best. Let go of the past. Apply the big five. Use a capable consultant. Appoint a strong interim pastor. Tie the search to the board. Look for the right track record. With momentum, consider succession, but not otherwise. Avoid conflicts of interest with interim and associate pastors. Tell the truth about the level of support.
Firing the lead pastor	Protect long tenure for effective pastors. Have a nondebatable reason. Tell the truth about the reason. Extend transitional support with impressive generosity.
Developing property and buildings	Use rented space as much as possible. Design facilities as multipurpose to a point. Use multiple services and sites to expand proactively. Relieve one pinch point at a time. Make prudent use of borrowed funds.
Creating annual budgets	Fund the essential mission outcomes first. Present the budget publicly in broad categories. Rely on staff to create the budget. Establish criteria in advance for an acceptable budget. Consider the option of leaving budget approval to the board.

Staffing for success	Hire an executive pastor. Supplement with part-time and contract staff. Invest in volunteer staff. Staff works for the lead pastor—period. Evaluate performance with integrity, based on prearranged expectations. Structure compensation strategically rather than conventionally.
Setting up the board	Keep a governance board small but not too small. Train and screen for agenda harmony. Unify behind majority decisions. Guard against conflicts of interest. Keep terms of service short.
Managing programs	Make all programming decisions at the staff level. Control the quality of essential services. Catalyze entrepreneurial outreach ministries. Put leadership development first. Attach every program to the Great Commission.
Maintaining bylaws	Fulfill outside mandates as flexibly as possible. Differentiate the essential roles and functions cleanly. Keep quorum and majority minimums easy to manage. Mandate very few meetings. Keep bylaws concise. Do your homework.
Managing membership	Create more than one commitment level. Tie membership to active service expectations. Integrate joining the church into a web of on-demand growth opportunities. Keep membership meetings aligned with God's mission and good pastoral leadership.

Exercising church discipline	Consider the option of renewable church membership. Invest generously in those who come clean. Protect the church decisively from those who resist correction.
Starting congregations	Combine multisite expansion and church planting. Reproduce at a bold but sustainable rate. Reproduce multipliers, not just mules.
Choosing mission partners	Go where the fish are biting. Combine a shotgun approach and a rifle approach. Choose partnerships that work in the twenty-first century.

Table 11.4 compiles all of the best practices discussed in the longest unit of the book, Chapter 9. Great congregations vary on the particulars, but as a whole these are the kinds of ways and means that better ministries use to yield wise decisions.

As for what not to do, Table 11.5 gathers the five top ten lists from the final chapter, "A Catalog of Dysfunctions to Avoid." By their very nature, these items are identified by their absence or opposite in healthy, growing churches.

TABLE 11.5—FIFTY DYSFUNCTIONS AT A GLANCE

Level	Dysfunctions
Congregation	Maintain confusing, overly detailed bylaws. Acquiesce to a big donor's questionable agenda. Use parliamentary procedure as the dominant feature of congregational meetings. Hold out for unanimity rather than unifying behind majority decisions. Maintain low expectations of leaders. Discuss sensitive details at the congregational level. Process difficult decisions in a single extended meeting. Give way to emotionally controlling personalities. Tolerate passive-aggressive behavior. Promote a "checks and balances" mind-set.
Board	Fail to screen for conflicts of interest. Confuse biblical titles with functional assignments. Treat stakeholders as if they were owners. Defer to "expertise" over agreed standards. Allow a vacuum in the office of lead pastor. Allow more than one line of accountability from staff. Triangulate information under the guise of protection. Set financial limits too low or too high. Engage with employee and "customer" complaints. Use consultants to deflect responsibility.
Lead Pastor	Pay too much or too little attention to precedent. Gloss over difficult problems. Conflate first-century practice with biblical teaching. Treat staff with a "neglect and zap" approach. Misuse development tools as evaluation tools. Assume an entitlement mentality. Put idealism ahead of pragmatism. Put pragmatism ahead of integrity. Succumb to paralysis by analysis. Fail to perform due diligence.

Staff	Fail to develop a winning team together. Angle for multiple or fuzzy lines of accountability. Fail to clarify expectations of performance. Move the goalposts during an evaluation. Work an agenda out of synch with the pastor's vision. Act like an expense rather than an investment. Triangulate with influencers. Fail to give and receive affirmation. Give more attention to weaknesses than to strengths. Neglect the needs and relationships of spouses.
Tribe	Pursue institutional aims over missional aims. Underestimate the potential of franchising. Keep the champions on the sidelines. Throw out the baby with the bathwater. Stick with the good old boy network. Ignore the big financial trends. Confuse the word *denomination* with its reality. Place pastors with little regard to their track record. Fail to let pastors prove themselves. Preserve strangleholds of historical polity.

A final caveat

As much as structures and practices affect decision making, people affect them more. Systems are not a substitute for leadership or for relationship. In fact, good leaders produce good systems, not the other way around. And the human dynamics do not disappear with growth or size.

Ray Johnston, lead pastor of Bayside Church, faced the need to lay off two senior associates one year. One was highly competent but had poor chemistry with the lead pastor and the team. The other had great relational chemistry but simply wasn't able to do the job. Both situations had been tolerated in the absence of financial pressure. Now they both had to go—with generous transitional support. Ironically, the high-competence pastor handled his departure graciously despite having been pegged as a man without relational strengths. The teddy bear pastor, however, acted out and tried to recruit sympathy among board members against the lead pastor. Fortunately, Ray's board stays out of staff decisions, and a congregation of ten thousand makes it hard to recruit much of a following for a personal power play.

Only a small handful of pastors and boards will serve a congregation with a five-figure attendance, of course. Knowing that personalities have a bearing even at that order of magnitude, however, offers a reality check for churches of every shape and size. So, when you leave the harbor "to fish for people," bring the best nets you can find, but don't forget that the right crew makes a difference when it's time to fish or cut bait.

Additional Resources

At the back of the book you'll find an appendix with a chart of ten winning churches, a bibliography, and a word about yours truly.

APPENDIX

Profiles of Ten Winning Churches

THE TEN WINNING CHURCHES PROFILED in chart form are displayed as a two-page spread. Each column is a feature. Each row is a congregation. The category of each one generally follows Lyle Schaller's breakdown by size range, except that no distinction is made between his "megachurch" and "mini-denomination" on the chart. Bayside and El Camino, each more than ten thousand people, would fall into the latter for Schaller. The column labeled "Lesson" contains what I believe a reader might most uniquely learn from each congregation. In some cases the descriptor is from the ministry's own literature; in other cases it is mine. Culture is straightforward for most of the congregations. Sometimes I had to make a judgment call on the descriptor that seemed most useful. Each church here has a website. Those addresses are provided (the text wrap is not intended to indicate a break in the web address), which, of course, will lead to full contact information if desired.

Lead Pastor	Category	Culture	Polity & Tribe	Location
Wooddale Church	Mega	Anglo +	Congregational Baptist—BGC	Eden Prairie, Minnesota
Église Baptiste Évangélique	Large	French Canadian	Congregational Baptist— Evangelical	Terrebonne-Mascouche, Quebec
Element 3 Church	Large	Anglo +	Congregational Nondenominational	Tallahassee, Florida
Richmond Emmanuel Church	Large	Chinese Canadian	Episcopal Anglican—AMiA	Richmond, British Columbia
Bayside Church	Mega	Anglo +	Congregational Evangelical Covenant	Granite Bay, California
Flipside Christian Church	Large	Anglo +	Congregational Baptist—GHC	Madera Ranchos, California
First Baptist Church	Very Large	Anglo +	Congregational Baptist—GHC	Clovis, California
Riverside Church	Very Large	Anglo +	Presb./Cong. Mix C&MA	Big Lake, Minnesota
Bedford Central Presbyterian	Large	African American & Caribbean	Presbyterian PCUSA	Brooklyn, New York
La Iglesia en El Camino	Mega	Latino	Episcopal Four Square Gospel	Santa Clarita, California

Lead Pastor	Setting	Region	Lesson	Website
Leith Anderson	Suburban	Midwest U.S.	Consistent excellence	wooddale.org
Louis Bourque	Suburban	Quebec	Evangelism and church planting	ebetm.org
Mark McNees	Suburban	Southern U.S.	Cultural engagement	element3.org
Silas Ng	Suburban	Pacific Coast	Courageous integrity	emmanuelvoice.org
Ray Johnston	Suburban	Northern California	High-impact legacy	baysideonline.com
Karl Roth	Small Town (near big city)	Central California	"Scandalous grace"	acts176.com
Tim Brown	Suburban	Central California	Community impact	fbclovis.com
Tom Lundeen	Small Town (near big city)	Midwest U.S.	Steady, credible leadership	myriversidechurch.com
Clive Neil	Urban	New York City	Community-centered ministry	bedfordcentral.org
Jaime Tolle	Suburban	Southern California	Evangelism through worship	laiglesiaenelcamino.org

Notes

Preface

1. See http://www.randomhouse.com/wotd/index.pperl?date=20010612, and http://www.phrases.org.uk/meanings/fish-or-cut-bait.html. Both accessed 29 January 2011.

2. "Come, follow me," Jesus said, "and I will send you out to fish for people" (Mark 1:17 TNIV).

3. *Antidisestablishmentarianism* is a word primarily known for its length. Its meaning, however, relates directly to church organization. It was the name of a movement in nineteenth-century Britain opposed to the disestablishment of the Church of England as the state religion. The movement lost in Ireland and won in England. By comparison, the "establishment clause" in the U.S. Bill of Rights was originally intended to disallow any one denomination as a national church.

Introduction

1. Christian Swartz, *Natural Church Development: A Guide to Eight Essential Qualities of Healthy Churches* (Carol Stream, IL: ChurchSmart Resources, 1996), 22–37.

2. Stephen Macchia, *Becoming a Healthy Church: 10 Characteristics* (Grand Rapids: Baker Books, 1999), 23.

3. Kennon Callahan, *Twelve Keys to an Effective Church: Strategic Planning for Mission* (San Francisco: Harper & Row, 1983), 118.

4. Rick Warren, *The Purpose-Driven Church: Growth without Compromising Your Message & Mission* (Grand Rapids: Zondervan, 1995), 49.

5. Leith Anderson, *A Church for the 21st Century: Bringing Change to Your Church to Meet the Challenges of a Changing Society* (Minneapolis: Bethany House, 1992), 123–42.

6. Mark Dever, *Nine Marks of a Healthy Church*, new expanded ed. (Wheaton, IL: Crossway Books, 2004), 29–31.

2. What Must Be Done?

1. George W. Bullard Jr., *Pursuing the Full Kingdom Potential of Your Congregation* (St. Louis: Lake Hickory Resources, 2005), 77–78; italics his. *FaithSoaring* is shorthand for what he calls a "spiritual strategic journey."

2. Ibid., 78.

3. Who Says So?

1. Story related by Leith Anderson in Niagara Falls, November 2009.

2. "Do not entertain an accusation against an elder unless it is brought by two or three witnesses. Those who sin are to be rebuked publicly, so that the others may take warning" (1 Timothy 5:19-20 NIV).

4. Who Takes the Lead?

1. Edgar Schein, *Organizational Culture and Leadership*, 4th ed. (San Francisco: Jossey-Bass, 2010), 244.

2. Lyle Schaller, *The Multiple Staff and the Larger Church* (Nashville: Abingdon Press, 1980), 41.

3. Leith Anderson, "How to Win at Parish Poker," *Leadership Journal* 7 (winter 1986). http://www.ctlibrary.com/le/1986/winter/86l1044.html. Accessed 10 March 2011.

5. What's It Going to Cost?

1. "This is to my Father's glory, that you bear much fruit, showing yourselves to be my disciples" (John 15:8).

2. Murray Moerman, ed., *Transforming Our Nation: Empowering the Canadian Church for a Greater Harvest* (Richmond, BC: Church Leadership Library, 1998), 260.

3. http://www.element3.org

6. What If There's Trouble?

1. George W. Bullard Jr., *Pursuing the Full Kingdom Potential of Your Congregation* (St. Louis: Lake Hickory Resources, 2005), 108–9.

2. "Wooddale Church Constitution, Revised February 2005," Article V. The story was shared in a public address in Niagara Falls, November 10, 2009.

7. The Art of Application

1. Kevin Freiberg and Jackie Freiberg, *Nuts: Southwest Airlines' Crazy Recipe for Business and Personal Success* (Austin: Bard Press, 1996), 90.

8. Who Decides What

1. The more generic terms of *pastor, board, council,* and *overseer* are used in place of the unique alternatives that vary among denominations, such as *rector, minister, session, vestry, presbytery, classis, synod, bishop,* and *superintendent.*

2. What is meant is the document that creates and defines the corporation. In the United States, this is known as the articles of incorporation. In Commonwealth countries, it may be known as letters patent.

3. John Maxwell, *The 21 Irrefutable Laws of Leadership* (Nashville: Thomas Nelson, 1998), 225.

4. See http://www.growinghealthychurches.org and http://www.ubahouston.org, respectively. Key books from these two judicatories are *Assaulting the Gates: Aiming All God's People at the Mission Field*, by Paul D. Borden (Nashville: Abingdon Press, 2009), and *Leading Congregational Change: A Practical Guide for the Transformational Journey*, by James H. Furr, Mike Bonem, and Jim Harrington (San Francisco: Jossey-Bass, 2000).

5. This Afghan proverb is attributed to John Maxwell because of his frequent use of it, but it is not original to him.

6. "What the CEO wants the board to do may be of interest and may even have some legitimate influence, but it is surely not the driving force of good governance." John

Carver, *Boards That Make a Difference: A New Design for Leadership in Nonprofit and Public Organizations*, 3rd ed. (San Francisco: Jossey-Bass, 2006), 173. My alternative to Carver's model, which I call "Accountable Leadership," is presented in *Winning on Purpose: Organizing Congregations to Succeed in Their Mission* (Nashville: Abingdon Press, 2006).

7. See Carver, *Boards That Make a Difference*.

8. See Kaiser, *Winning on Purpose*.

9. "Amended and Restated Bylaw of Saddleback Valley Community Church (as of May 21, 1997), a California Nonprofit Religious Corporation," Article VII.

10. Not much financial conflict of interest remains for Warren himself. In 2005 he made news by going off the payroll and returning all the salary he had received from the church over the previous twenty-five years. See Timothy C. Morgan, "Purpose Driven in Rwanda: Rick Warren's Sweeping Plan to Defeat Poverty," *Christianity Today* 49 (October 2005). http://www.christianitytoday.com/ct/2005/october/17.32.html. Accessed 21 January 2011.

11. See Edwin H. Friedman, *Generation to Generation: Family Process in Church and Synagogue* (New York: Guilford Press, 1985).

9. Best Practices for Typical Decisions

1. Thom S. Rainer, *Breakout Churches: Discover How to Make the Leap* (Grand Rapids: Zondervan, 2005), 56–57.

2. This observation may seem foreign to many congregations, but it is actually an understatement. In fact, virtually none of the healthy, growing churches named as positive examples in *Fish or Cut Bait* have ever pressured a lead pastor to leave, a fact that speaks volumes. The only possible exceptions would be the "before picture" days of a turn-around situation when a church would not have qualified for the list. The best practices offered on this point have mostly to do with what has kept excellent congregations from going off the rails with their pastor.

3. http://www.enewhope.org/index.php/locations/. Accessed 23 Jan 2011. I suppose my favorite one should probably be the Oahu campus at Kaiser High School!

4. Generous severance was provided from cash reserves.

5. In the history of the United States, the House of Representatives has impeached two presidents, Andrew Johnson and Bill Clinton. (Richard Nixon resigned prior to an expected impeachment.) In both cases a majority of senators voted to convict but failed to achieve the supermajority required. The resulting political stalemate lasted until the end of each man's term of office.

6. The church in Nevada, then, might use the following wording to protect its freedom to design the membership concept as it sees fit: "The congregation shall be considered church members as defined in these bylaws; the church shall have no statutory members as defined in Nevada state law (NRS 82.031)." Whereas the church in California might accomplish the same flexibility for itself with these words: "The congregation shall be considered church members as defined in these bylaws; as provided in the California Corporations Code (CCC 9330, 9511-12). Membership shall entail no definitions, rights, or responsibilities other than those explicitly stated in these bylaws." Please note that this information does not constitute legal advice and should not be relied upon as such. Always consult an attorney for legal advice.

7. For example, Wooddale Church's "fellowship members." In "Wooddale Church Constitution, Revised February 2005," Article V.

8. First Baptist Church of Clovis Bylaws, Section 5.

9. For example, the U.S. Center for World Mission provides strategic updated information on the state of unreached people groups at http://www.uscwm.org, and the Evangelical Council for Financial Accountability (http//www.ecfa.org) in the United States and the Canadian Council of Christian Charities (http://www.cccc.org) in Canada provide information on the financial practices of mission organizations in those countries.

10. Also see detailed best-practice chart in the conclusion.

10. A Catalog of Dysfunctions to Avoid

1. The thesis of *Governance Matters: Balancing Client and Staff Fulfillment in Faith-Based Not-for-Profit Organizations* by Les Stahlke with Jennifer Loughlin (Edmonton: GovernanceMatters.com, 2003) is that the interests of two groups of stakeholders (staff and clients) should determine the course of an organization. The book has helpful ideas for serving staff and clients, but its weakness is that it neglects the ownership of an organization. For a congregation, that ownership is Christ, transmitting his agenda as understood through polity. A congregation's staff or "clients" may want something different.

2. For example, Proverbs 17:9; 24:2; Matthew 5:23-24; 18:15-17; Ephesians 5:19-20; James 3:5; 4:11.

3. See John Carver, *Boards That Make a Difference*, 3rd ed. (San Francisco: Jossey-Bass, 2006), 174–76; John Edmund Kaiser, *Winning on Purpose* (Nashville: Abingdon Press, 2006), 124; and Jim Brown, *The Imperfect Board Member* (San Francisco: Jossey-Bass, 2006), 28–41.

4. See David L. Dotlich and Peter C. Cairo, *Why CEOs Fail: The 11 Behaviors That Can Derail Your Climb to the Top—and How to Manage Them* (San Francisco: Jossey-Bass, 2003), 64–75.

5. Used in private for professional growth, 360-degree feedback is invaluable. Three-hundred-sixty-degree feedback used for a performance review not only changes the criteria for performance after the fact but the de facto supervisors as well (to include peers and subordinates). One international mission director, who lost his job after two unhappy subordinates sabotaged him in this manner, said he felt as if his board had handed disgruntled staff a machine gun.

6. See Jim Griffith and Bill Easum, *Ten Most Common Mistakes Made by New Church Starts* (St. Louis: Chalice Press, 2008), 21–31.

7. A description used by psychologist Larry Crabb.

8. Patrick Lencioni, *The Five Dysfunctions of a Team: A Leadership Fable* (San Francisco, 2002).

9. Cf., Warren Bennis and Burt Nanus, *Leaders: The Strategies for Taking Charge* (New York: Harper & Row, 1985), 56–62; and Tom Rath and Barry Conchie, *Strengths-Based Leadership: Great Leaders, Teams, and Why People Follow* (New York: Gallup Press, 2008), 7–17.

10. See Teresa Flint-Borden and Barbara Cooper, *Women Married to Men in Ministry: Breaking the Sound Barrier Together* (Nashville: Abingdon Press, 2007).

Conclusion

1. Jim Collins, *Good to Great: Why Some Companies Make the Leap . . . and Others Don't* (New York: HarperBusiness, 2001).

Bibliography

Anderson, Leith. *A Church for the 21st Century: Bringing Change to Your Church to Meet the Challenges of a Changing Society*. Minneapolis: Bethany House, 1992.

Bennis, Warren, and Burt Nanus. *Leaders: The Strategies for Taking Charge*. New York: Harper & Row, 1985.

Borden, Paul D. *Assaulting the Gates: Aiming All God's People at the Mission Field*. Nashville: Abingdon Press, 2009.

Brown, Jim. *The Imperfect Board Member: Discovering the Seven Disciplines of Governance Excellence*. San Francisco: Jossey-Bass, 2006.

Bullard, George W., Jr. *Pursuing the Full Kingdom Potential of Your Congregation*. St. Louis, MO: Lake Hickory Resources, 2005.

Callahan, Kennon L. *Twelve Keys to an Effective Church: Strategic Planning for Mission*. San Francisco: Harper & Row, 1983.

Carver, John. *Boards That Make a Difference: A New Design for Leadership in Nonprofit and Public Organizations*. 3rd ed. San Francisco: Jossey-Bass, 2006.

Collins, Jim. *Good to Great: Why Some Companies Make the Leap . . . and Others Don't*. New York: HarperBusiness, 2001.

Dever, Mark. *Nine Marks of a Healthy Church*. New expanded ed. Wheaton, IL: Crossway Books, 2004.

Dotlich, David L., and Peter C. Cairo. *Why CEOs Fail: The 11 Behaviors That Can Derail Your Climb to the Top—and How to Manage Them*. San Francisco: Jossey-Bass, 2003.

Flint-Borden, Teresa, and Barbara Cooper. *Women Married to Men in Ministry: Breaking the Sound Barrier Together*. Nashville: Abingdon Press, 2007.

Freiberg, Kevin, and Jackie Freiberg. *Nuts: Southwest Airlines' Crazy Recipe for Business and Personal Success*. Austin: Bard Press, 1996.

Friedman, Edwin H. *Generation to Generation: Family Process in Church and Synagogue*. New York: Guilford Press, 1985.

Furr, James H., Mike Bonem, and Jim Harrington. *Leading Congregational Change: A Practical Guide for the Transformational Journey.* San Francisco: Jossey-Bass, 2000.

Griffith, Jim, and Bill Easum. *Ten Most Common Mistakes Made by New Church Starts.* St. Louis: Chalice Press, 2008.

Kaiser, John Edmund. *Winning on Purpose: How to Organize Congregations to Succeed in Their Mission.* Nashville: Abingdon Press, 2006.

Lencioni, Patrick. *The Five Dysfunctions of a Team: A Leadership Fable.* San Francisco: Jossey-Bass, 2002.

Macchia, Stephen A. *Becoming a Healthy Church: 10 Characteristics.* Grand Rapids: Baker Books, 1999.

Maxwell, John. *The 21 Irrefutable Laws of Leadership: Follow Them and People Will Follow You.* Nashville: Thomas Nelson, 1998.

Moerman, Murray, ed., *Transforming Our Nation: Empowering the Canadian Church for a Greater Harvest.* Richmond, BC: Church Leadership Library, 1998.

Rainer, Thom S. *Breakout Churches: Discover How to Make the Leap.* Grand Rapids: Zondervan, 2005.

Rath, Tom, and Barry Conchie. *Strengths Based Leadership: Great Leaders, Teams, and Why People Follow.* New York: Gallup Press, 2008.

Schaller, Lyle. *The Multiple Staff and the Larger Church.* Nashville: Abingdon Press, 1980.

Schein, Edgar H. *Organizational Culture and Leadership.* 4th ed. San Francisco: Jossey-Bass, 2010.

Stahlke, Les, with Jennifer Loughlin. *Governance Matters: Balancing Client and Staff Fulfillment in Faith-Based Not-for-Profit Organizations.* Edmonton: GovernanceMatters.com, 2003.

Swartz, Christian A. *Natural Church Development: A Guide to Eight Essential Qualities of Healthy Churches.* Carol Stream, IL: ChurchSmart Resources, 1996.

Warren, Rick. *The Purpose-Driven Church: Growth without Compromising Your Message & Mission.* Grand Rapids: Zondervan, 1995.

About the Author

John E. Kaiser

John Kaiser is a writer, consultant, and executive coach. In more than thirty years of professional ministry, he has taught college and seminary courses, planted churches, led a large multistaff church, directed a church planting movement, trained boards, assessed congregations, coached pastors, and served as president of a denomination.

He has worked extensively across the United States and Canada, and from time to time in Australia and New Zealand. His undergraduate degree is from Bryan College; his two master's degrees are from Trinity Evangelical Divinity School; and his doctorate is from Denver Seminary.

He and Leonore, his wife of thirty-two years, live in Ontario, Canada. They enjoy their adult children (Ben and wife Katrina, and Ruth), their young grandchildren (Owen and Ellie), and each other.

Check out http://www.accountableleadership.org.

59588362R00099

Made in the USA
Lexington, KY
10 January 2017